Guided Reading Library
Teacher's Manual

Grade 1

Harcourt

Orlando   Boston   Dallas   Chicago   San Diego

Visit *The Learning Site!*
www.harcourtschool.com

The Conversion Chart is intended to help teachers in purchasing leveled books from Harcourt. Please note the following:

(1) Reading Recovery® is a registered service mark of The Ohio State University.
(2) The complete Reading Recovery® book list, created by the Reading Recovery® Council of North America, includes books from numerous publishers since a premise of the program is that children be provided with a range of texts. One publisher's book list alone is not sufficient to implement a Reading Recovery® program.
(3) Levels are subject to change as they are periodically tested and reevaluated.

Printed in the United States of America

ISBN 0-15-319196-1

7 8 9 10 11 12 073 2010 2009 2008 2007 2006 2005

Contents

GUIDED READING

What is Guided Reading?

Guided reading provides an opportunity for teacher-guided instruction. Guided reading is reading by students in small groups on their instructional level with the teacher acting as a facilitator, prompting and assisting each student. The groups of 4–6 students are homogeneous, and students share a topic as they learn and apply reading strategies. Guided reading groups change frequently based on the teacher's ongoing assessment of reading levels and students' understanding of strategies.

Characteristics of Guided Reading

1. Students are grouped according to their instructional level.
2. This small group of students will read a leveled text.
3. The teacher presents a book introduction.
4. While students read independently, the teacher checks individual students for understanding and application of strategies, and offers prompts to help them apply strategies to problem solve.
5. After reading, the teacher checks comprehension through a retelling and/or discussion, reviews the problem-solving strategies used, and may have students reread for fluency.
6. The teacher may take a student aside at any time to do an individual reading inventory to determine whether the student's level has changed.

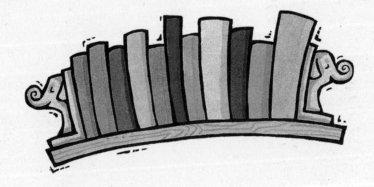

Role of the Teacher

BEFORE READING

- Groups the students in small groups of 4–6.
- Selects the text that is at the appropriate level.
- Introduces the book, accesses prior knowledge, and helps students determine a purpose for reading.

DURING READING

- Observes strategies individual students use.
- Offers support to help students problem-solve the text.
- Records observations.

AFTER READING

- Discusses the story selection.
- Returns to the text to review problem-solving strategies.
- May offer an opportunity to reread for fluency and for additional practice applying strategies.
- Assesses students to evaluate reading level changes.

Role of the Student

BEFORE READING

- Provides comments and responses during the book introduction.
- Sets a purpose for reading.

DURING READING

- Reads the entire text.
- Uses problem-solving strategies to comprehend.
- Requests teacher support as needed.
- Demonstrates understanding through discussion with the teacher.

AFTER READING

- Discusses the story with the group.
- Revisits the text to analyze problem-solving strategies.
- May reread the story to apply strategies and develop fluency.

How to Conduct a Guided Reading Session

TEACHER PLANNING

Know your students.

It's important that each student's reading level and knowledge of strategies are established in order to organize students into homogeneous groups. **Taking an individual reading inventory** will help you determine each student's instructional reading level. Observing a student's reading will also familiarize you with the reader's understanding of print and the strategies with which he or she is familiar. Information about how to determine your students' levels can be found on pages 8–11.

Know the text.

Be familiar with the book and **know the book's level.** Leveling information can be found on page 8. Determine how much background students may have on the topic to help decide whether students will be able to understand the concepts and whether they will find the topic interesting.

Present a book introduction.

A good book introduction will **motivate students, tap their prior knowledge, and introduce difficult concepts and words.** Read the title to students or have them read the title to you. Ask a question to tap prior knowledge. Take a **picture walk** through the book, pointing out text features, encouraging speculation and predictions, inviting connections, discussing difficult concepts or unfamiliar vocabulary, and getting students started using some of the story language. The purpose of a book introduction is to prepare students to read using the strategies they are practicing and applying to help them be successful with the text.

Observe students.

During the reading, **observe students** and work with individuals to determine whether they are **using problem-solving strategies.**

Use prompts.

The following prompts may be used to coach students and to provide scaffolding needed to help them problem solve.

A. *Structure*

You said _____. Does that sound right?

Can you say it that way?

Does it sound good to your ear?

B. *Visual*

You said _____. Does it look right?

What sound can you see in that word?

What would you expect to see at the beginning? at the end? after the _____?

C. *Cross-Checking*

It could be _____, but look at it.

Check to see if what you read looks right and sounds right to you.

You made a mistake on that page. Can you find it?

I like the way you found out what was wrong all by yourself.

D. *Meaning*

You said _____. Does that make sense?

Look at the picture.

Do you remember when that happened in the story before?

What is happening now?

As students become more advanced in their use of word solving strategies, they will need to shift their attention to **comprehending to problem solve**. Here are additional strategies they will need:

E. *Rereading*

Do you remember what happened before _____?

What will help you remember what happened on pages _____ and _____?

If you reread pages _____ and _____, how do you think that will help you?

Do you know what that word means?

What can you do to help yourself understand it?

F. *Summarize and Predict*

Think about the __(3)__ most important things that happened so far. What are they?

What do you think will happen next?

G. *Self-Question*

Do you know why this happened?

What can you ask yourself to help you understand?

Strategies Good Readers Use

The following are strategies that are taught and reinforced throughout *Collections*. These strategies are also taught and reinforced in this manual.

- **Look for Words You Know.** Find words you know. Use those words to help you figure out the words you don't know.

- **Look for Word Bits and Parts.** When you see a word you don't know, look for parts of the word that are familiar.

- **Self-Correct.** Sometimes you need to change the way you read something so that it makes sense.

- **Read Ahead.** When you get to a word you have tried to sound out but still don't know, try reading ahead. Or, if you are having trouble understanding something in a selection, keep on reading. The meaning may become clear when you have more information.

- **Reread Aloud.** Sometimes you can figure out a tricky word when you reread out loud the sentences that are before the word.

- **Reread.** If something doesn't make sense, you may have missed an important point. Try rereading an earlier part of the selection.

- **Use Picture Clues to Confirm Meaning.** Look at the pictures to help you understand what the words say.

- **Use Context to Confirm Meaning.** After you read an unfamiliar or difficult word, ask yourself whether what you read makes sense in the sentence and whether it fits what is happening in the selection.

- **Make and Confirm Predictions.** Think about what might happen next. Read to find out whether you are right. Make new predictions as you read.

- **Sequence Events/Summarize.** Think about the order in which things happen. When you finish reading, see if you can tell about the main things that happened.

- **Summarize.** Tell or list the main points of the selection or the main things that happened. This will help you understand and remember what you read.

- **Create Mental Images.** Sometimes, picturing in your mind what you are reading can help you understand and enjoy a selection. Pay attention to descriptive details.

- **Make Inferences.** An author doesn't tell everything. Often, the author shows things and lets the reader decide what they mean. As you read, look for clues that help you figure out what the words don't say.

Using Guided Reading Groups with *Collections*

Working with small groups often presents management problems in the classroom. The most important question teachers ask is

**What are the other students in my class doing
while I work with a Guided Reading group?**

PRIMARY GRADES The chart below offers suggestions for working with a Guided Reading group in the primary grades while using *Collections*.

RED GROUP	BLUE GROUP	YELLOW GROUP
Guided Reading Group	Writing Center	Letter and Word Center
At My Desk (Completing *Practice Book* pages or doing Word Builder activities)	Guided Reading Group	Social Studies Center
Letter and Word Center	At My Desk (Completing *Practice Book* pages or working in writing folder)	Guided Reading Group
Art Center	Social Studies Center	At My Desk (Building words with Letter Cards)

INTERMEDIATE GRADES The chart below offers suggestions for working with a Guided Reading group in the intermediate grades while using *Collections*.

RED GROUP	BLUE GROUP	YELLOW GROUP
Guided Reading Group	Research Station (Completing a Cross-Curricular activity)	Listening Station (Listening to a selection)
At My Desk (Completing a *Practice Book* assignment or writing in journals)	Guided Reading Group	Computer Station (Publishing or using a CD-ROM)
Art Station (Completing a Building Literacy Skills activity)	At My Desk (Completing *Practice Book* assignment or Writing assignment)	Guided Reading Group

Classroom Management

There are several ways to use the *Collections* Student Editions along with the *Collections* Guided Reading Library:

1. As groups of students read the *Collections* Student Edition selection, use the Guided Reading notes in the Teacher's Edition to teach and reinforce "Strategies Good Readers Use." After that initial instruction, small groups can work in Guided Reading groups to apply the strategies they learned. Students can use *Take-Home Books, Leveled Library* books, or *Reader's Choice Library* books.

2. While some students read the *Collections* Student Edition selection independently, work with other students in Guided Reading groups using the *Take-Home Books, Leveled Library* books, or *Reader's Choice Library* books.

3. After students who are working at their instructional level read and respond to a *Collections* Student Edition selection, have them work in a designated center or station completing a Building Literacy Skills activity or a Cross-Curricular activity. Those students who need instruction in or additional reinforcement of guided reading strategies will work in a Guided Reading group using a *Take-Home Book, Leveled Library* book, or a *Reader's Choice Library* book.

Leveling

WHAT ARE LEVELED BOOKS?

Grade 1

Grades 2-6

Leveled books are specific books that have been sequenced for difficulty using a consistent formula across all grades. Leveled books make it possible to match students to texts with which they will be successful. A book level is only an *approximate* indicator of difficulty. A new level may be assigned to a book at any time if teachers agree it belongs at another level.

Collections Leveled Library books including *Reader's Choice Library* books have been leveled for your convenience. Level designations have been assigned and appear on the back of the books. To the left are examples.

HOW THE BOOKS WERE LEVELED

Primary Grades   These characteristics were included in the leveling process:
- content
- illustrations
- vocabulary
- repetition of language patterns
- language structures
- narrative structure
- text position

Intermediate Grades   The criteria are expanded to include:
- prior knowledge
- vocabulary and concept load
- amount of text
- length of book
- text structure
- genre
- illustration support

Benchmark Books

What are Benchmark Books?

Benchmark Books are leveled books that can be used to determine students' reading levels. For each level, Benchmark Books have been identified to assist in matching students to those texts with which they will be most successful. Benchmark Books, along with the appropriate assessment data, will help to determine what students are capable of reading, what they are ready to learn, and how to group them most effectively for instruction.

DETERMINING YOUR STUDENTS' LEVELS

Benchmark Books can be used for evaluation.

For each book, two forms are included. The first form gives information about the book, the number of words, a reading passage, and comprehension questions. The second is a form for taking a summary.

Use at each evaluation point.

The book can be presented with an introduction and by having the student look at the cover, read the title, and make predictions about what he or she will read. Then the student reads the book aloud. (In later grades, students will read passages from books, rather than complete books.) The student's miscues are recorded on the record form. Questions are provided to assess comprehension. If the book is at the student's instructional level, he or she will score with 90–95 percent accuracy on the word recognition task and 80 percent accuracy on the comprehension task.

Use for retellings.

Guidelines for performing a retelling evaluation, as well as a rubric for scoring a retelling, are provided on pages 10–11 of this manual. If both a retelling and questions are used, the student should retell the story first.

Determine a student's level.

If the student meets the benchmark, he or she is ready for instruction at the next level. If the student has too many errors or reads the book with almost perfect accuracy, reassess at a lower or higher level to find the student's instructional level. Students at the same level can be assigned to guided reading groups.

Marking Oral Reading Miscues

READING MISCUE	MARKING	SAMPLE
1. Omissions	Circle the word, word part, or phrase omitted.	I will let you ⊙go⊙ in.
2. Insertions	Insert a caret (^) and write in the inserted word or phrase.	big We bought a ^parrot.
3. Substitutions	Write the word or phrase the student substitutes above the word or phrase in the text.	the Dad fixed ~~my~~ bike.
4. Mispronunciations	Write the phonetic mispronunciation above the word.	feed Have you ~~fed~~ the dog?
5. Self-corrections	Write the letters *SC* next to the miscue that is self-corrected.	spot We took our ~~space~~. SC
6. Repetitions	Draw a line under any part of the text that is repeated.	It is your <u>garden</u> now.
7. Punctuation	Circle punctuation missed. Write in any punctuation inserted.	Take them home⊙ Then come back ^ and you and I will go to town.
8. Hesitations	Place vertical lines at places where the student hesitates excessively.	Pretend/this is mine.

Using Retelling to Assess Comprehension

RETELLING

Retelling is an assessment strategy that may be used to measure a student's strengths and weaknesses in comprehension. Listening to a retelling provides insights into a student's ability to construct meaning, to identify important information, to make inferences, and to organize and summarize information. Specifically, a retelling can assess whether the student

- relates the main idea and relevant details in sequence
- provides a summarizing statement
- includes story elements
- uses phrases, language, or vocabulary from the text
- evaluates an author's point of view, purpose, or craft
- stays on topic
- understands relationships in the text
- provides extensions of the text
- relates text to relevant experiences

ORAL RETELLING

When conducting an oral retelling, ask students to tell the story in their own words. Try not to interrupt. Allow plenty of time for a student to complete an oral retelling, and be sure the student has nothing more to say before ending the session.

For the emerging reader, reading books with limited text, the retelling may be short and fairly simple. For more complex books, if a student needs prompting, try using generic statements such as "Tell me more." If you need to elicit more information, prompt the student by asking open-ended questions such as:

- What was the character's main problem?
- What was your favorite part of the story?
- Where did the story take place?
- Who else was in the story?
- How did the story end?
- What else do you remember from the story?

WRITTEN RETELLING

When conducting a written retelling, ask students to tell the story in their own words and not to worry about spelling or handwriting. Try to allow plenty of time for students to complete writing before ending the session.

Use the rubric on page 11 to assess oral and written retellings.

Scoring Rubric for Retellings

SCORE	CHARACTERISTICS
3	**Proficient: Student retells the text using complex responses that demonstrate a thorough understanding and interpretation of the text.** • relates the main idea and important and supporting details • relates text in sequence • provides a summarizing statement • includes story elements such as setting, characters, plot, problems, and resolutions • uses phrases, language, vocabulary, sentence structure, or literary devices from the text • evaluates the author's point of view, purpose, or craft • stays on topic • discriminates between reality and fantasy, fact and fiction • understands relationships in text such as cause and effect • classifies, groups, compares, or contrasts information • provides extensions of the text such as making connections to other texts, relating relevant experiences, or making generalizations
2	**Satisfactory: Student adequately retells the text and demonstrates an understanding of the text.** • relates the main idea and relevant details • relates most of the text in sequence • includes story elements such as setting, characters, main problem, and resolution • uses language or vocabulary from the text • stays on topic • discriminates between reality and fantasy • understands relationships in text such as cause and effect • classifies, groups, compares, or contrasts information • provides some extensions of the text such as making connections to other texts or relating relevant experiences
1	**Minimal: Student makes several inaccurate, incomplete, or irrelevant statements or otherwise provides evidence of lack of comprehension.** • misunderstands main idea and omits important details • relates text out of sequence • omits story elements or provides incorrect information about setting, characters, and plot • provides a poorly organized or unclear structure • provides no extensions of the text

Conversion Chart

BOOK TITLE	LEVELED LIBRARY LEVEL	READING RECOVERY® LEVEL	GUIDED READING LEVEL	LEXILE LEVEL
The Three Bears	Emergent	Wordless		
A Day at School	Emergent	1	A	
At Home	Emergent	1	A	
My book*	Emergent	1	A	
The Pet Store	Emergent	1	A	
All Fall Down	Emergent	1-2	A	
Butterflies	Emergent	1-2	A	
Garden Birthday	Emergent	1-2	A	N/A
My Dog	Emergent	1-2	A	
Old MacDonald's Fun Time Farm	Emergent	1-2	A	
The Baby	Emergent	1-2	A	N/A
What a Shower!	Emergent	1-2	A	
Have You Seen My Cat?	Emergent	2	A	
Good-bye, Fox	Emergent	2-3	B	N/A
I Like Food	Emergent	2-3	B	
Just Like You!	Emergent	2-3	B	N/A
My Sister Is My Friend	Emergent	2-3	B	80
Spring Pops Up	Emergent	2-3	B	
The Perfect Pet	Emergent	2-3	B	
We Are Friends	Emergent	2-3	B	
What Could It Be?	Emergent	2-3	B	N/A
Where Babies Play	Emergent	2-3	B	N/A
Bird's Bad Day	Emergent	3-4	B	
"Help!" Said Jed	Emergent	3-4	B	
Friendship Salad	Emergent	3-4	B	N/A
My Family Band	Emergent	3-4	B	150
One More Time	Emergent	3-4	B	
Play Ball!	Emergent	3-4	B	
What Time Is It?	Emergent	3-4	B	N/A
Five Little Ducks*	Emergent	4-5	B-D	
After Goldilocks	Emergent	5-6	C-D	N/A
Know Your Birthday Manners	Emergent	5-6	C-D	N/A
Happy Birthday	Early	6	C-D	
Sid and Sam	Early	6	C-D	
One Little Slip	Early	6-7	C-D	
Today Is Monday	Early	7-8	E	N/A
What Is in the Box?	Early	7-8	E	
Famous Feet	Early	7-8	E	
Five Little Monkeys Jumping on the Bed	Early	7-8	E	
"Pardon?" Said the Giraffe*	Early	9	F	
All I Did	Early	8-9	F	
Pet Day	Early	8-9	F	180
Four Very Big Beans	Early	8-9	F	
Look What I Can Read!	Early	8-9	F	130
Every Cat	Early	8-10	F	380
A Place for Nicholas	Early	9-10	F	
Frog's Day	Early	9-10	F	
Lost and Found	Early	9-10	F	N/A
My Wild Woolly	Early	9-10	F	10

BOOK TITLE	LEVELED LIBRARY LEVEL	READING RECOVERY® LEVEL	GUIDED READING LEVEL	LEXILE LEVEL
The King Who Loved to Dance	Early	9-10	F	370
The Little Chicks Sing	Early	9-10	F	80
The Night Walk	Early	9-10	F	N/A
What's Up?	Early	9-10	F	60
Let's Visit the Moon	Early	9-11	G	10
I Was Just About to Go to Bed	Early	10-11	G	240
The Green Grass Grows All Around	Early	10-11	G	N/A
Red	Early	10-11	G	190
Big Brown Bear	Early	10-12	G	
Alien Vacation	Early	11-12	G	N/A
Biscuit	Early	11-12	G	
Dancing	Early	11-12	G	
Green, Green, Green	Early	11-12	G	530
Two Bear Cubs*	Early	13	H	
Slowpoke Snail	Early	12-13	G-H	210
Lunch in Space	Early	12-14	G-H	270
Pet Riddles and Jokes with Franny and Frank	Early	12-14	G-H	30
Davy Crockett and the Wild Cat	Early	13-14	H	150
If You Were a Bat	Early	13-14	H	170
Plenty of Pets	Early	13-14	H	290
Dream Around the World	Early	13-14	H	160
Henry	Early	13-14	H	N/A
How 100 Dandelions Grew	Early	13-14	H	150
Silly Aunt Tilly	Fluent	14-15	H-I	210
How to Make a Lion Mask	Fluent	15-16	G-I	240
Shoe Town	Fluent	15-16	G-I	450
Skimper-Scamper	Fluent	15-16	G-I	220
Leo the Late Bloomer*	Fluent	16		120
Clean-Up Day	Fluent	16-17	I-J	500
Fire Fighters	Fluent	16-17	I-J	410
How the Sky Got Its Stars	Fluent	16-17	I-J	230
What's New at the Zoo?	Fluent	16-17	I-J	130
Ask Mr. Bear	Fluent	17	I-J	400
Hare's Big Tug-of-War	Fluent	17-18	I-J	250
The Big Dipper	Fluent	17-18	I-J	460
The Strongest One of All	Fluent	17-18	I-J	360
Peeping and Sleeping	Fluent	18-19	I-J	
Leon and Bob	Fluent	18	J-K	400
Little Fox Goes to the End of the World	Fluent	18	J-K	190
Four Fur Feet	Fluent	20+	J-K	
Henry and Mudge and the Happy Cat	Fluent	20+	J-K	470
How a Seed Grows	Fluent	20+	J-K	400
Listen Buddy	Fluent	20+	J-K	520
Man on the Moon	Fluent	20+	J-K	230
The Art Lesson*	Fluent	20+	M	650

*Benchmark Book

Reading Behaviors

GRADE 1

- Knows that print carries meaning
- Knows how print works: directionality (left to right, front to back), front to back of book, concept of words
- Knows where to begin reading
- Can follow or track a line of print
- Notices and interprets details in pictures
- Notices and uses language patterns in text
- Understands that spoken language is composed of sequences of sounds and that those sounds are represented by letters
- Begins to accumulate a reading vocabulary that includes high-frequency words
- Uses letter-sound correspondences to decode words
- Becomes a skillful, independent decoder who practices knowledge of sounds and letters in simple text

GRADE 2

- Uses a variety of strategies to support knowledge of letter-sound correspondences to identify and figure out new words—including use of context, word parts, familiar words, and letter patterns
- Decodes unfamiliar or new words independently, using known phonic elements, and syntactic and semantic cues
- Makes meaningful substitutions when reading
- Begins self-monitoring when reading by noticing mismatches in meaning or language
- Uses patterns, punctuation, and syntax to read with phrasing
- Moves fluently through text while reading for meaning
- Rereads to confirm meaning or to problem solve
- Self-corrects using meaning information and knowledge of decoding strategies

GRADE 3

- Effectively tracks print with eyes rather than finger or marker
- Reads fluently while focusing on meaning
- Rereads to check, confirm, and search for answers and clues when problem solving
- Uses known words to figure out the meaning of unknown words
- Uses text rather than relying on illustrations for constructing meaning

- Uses decoding, context, known words, and parts of words to figure out unknown words, following up with a check for meaning
- Checks on own reading and self-corrects, using a variety of strategies
- Effectively manages a variety of texts—including fiction and nonfiction

GRADE 4

- Reads for a variety of purposes—to learn, to problem solve, to identify with characters, to suspend himself or herself in time, to be surprised and then reassured
- Sustains interest and fluent reading through longer texts
- Comes back to a text if it requires more than one sitting to read
- Problem solves unfamiliar words or concepts without detracting from meaning
- Self-corrects internally when necessary to support meaning, but continues to move through text
- Reads silently
- Monitors own understanding while reading silently and knows what to do when comprehension breaks down

GRADE 5

- Reads silently for extended periods of time
- Reads extended texts—including chapter books
- Decodes competently, but also uses references to identify words or clarify word meanings
- Adjusts reading rate depending on purpose for reading and type of text
- Reads with a sense of whether or not he or she understands the text
- Applies a variety of strategies when comprehension breaks down—rereading, using format features, interpreting graphics, asking questions, using other texts
- Reads material at appropriate level without assistance
- Prefers silent reading

GRADE 6

- Chooses to read appropriate-level texts independently
- Reads extended texts—including novels
- Establishes purpose; adjusts reading rate and strategies depending on genre and purpose
- Uses cuing systems—semantic, syntactic, and graphophonic—to understand unfamiliar words
- Monitors comprehension effectively; applies a variety of strategies when comprehension breaks down
- Understands and appreciates authors' use of a variety of literary devices
- Identifies, relates, and compares information from a variety of sources

The Three Bears

retold by Kurt Nagahori

Summary

While the bear family is out for a walk, a girl stops by and makes herself at home in their house. Because many children are familiar with the story of Goldilocks and the Three Bears, this wordless version is a good one for readers at any level to share.

Introduce the Book

PREPARE TO READ Show the cover and have children use picture clues to read the title. Invite them to share what they know about this story. Preview each page and discuss what is happening. Ask children what is missing from this book. Have readers use "story language" to tell the story. **SET PURPOSE**

Guided Reading

Pages 2–3 **FOCUS STRATEGY** *Make Inferences* Ask children who the characters are. (*Goldilocks; Papa, Mama, Baby Bear*) Ask them how they know. Elicit or explain that they use picture clues and experience with the story to make inferences (good guesses or conclusions) about things the author has not told them.

Page 9 **FOCUS STRATEGY** *Use Picture Clues to Confirm Meaning* Have children tell what Goldilocks thinks of the porridge in each picture. Ask them how they know. Explain that even when a story has words, readers can still use the pictures to help them understand the story.

Pages 12–13 **FOCUS STRATEGY** *Make Inferences* Ask children whose bed Goldilocks falls asleep in. Ask how they can be sure. Guide them in looking at the pictures for clues that tell which bed she is in.

Monitor Comprehension

1. **How do the bears know someone has been in their house?** (*Possible response: They see Baby Bear's empty bowl and broken chair.*) **INFERENTIAL: DRAW CONCLUSIONS**

2. **How do you think Goldilocks feels at the end of the story? Will she go back to the bears' house?** (*Possible responses: She feels scared, glad to get away, maybe sorry about breaking the bears' things; I don't think she will go back.*) **INFERENTIAL: DETERMINE CHARACTERS' EMOTIONS**

3. **How do you like this book, especially compared to other stories of Goldilocks and the Three Bears? Give reasons.** (*Responses will vary.*) **CRITICAL: MAKE JUDGMENTS**

Write in Response to Reading

Have children draw and write about something they like to taste, smell, or feel. For example: *My bed feels cozy and safe.*

My book

by Ron Maris

Summary

The reader follows a cat through the gate, in the door, and on a tour of the house. The cat enters a bedroom, where a child is in bed reading a book—the same book the reader is reading. The story is told in pictures, with few words.

Introduce the Book

PREPARE TO READ Have a volunteer read the title. Let children guess whose book it is, using details on the cover. Read the title page and introduce the author/illustrator. On the next page, ask: **Is this the cat from the cover? Where is it going?** Read the next page to find out. Invite children to guess what lies behind the flap. Continue reading to find out where the cat goes. **SET PURPOSE**

Guided Reading

Page 3 **FOCUS STRATEGY** *Look for Words You Know* Use prompts to help children read unfamiliar words: **Do you know a word that looks like this? What do you know that might help?**

Pages 5–6 **FOCUS STRATEGY** *Use Context Clues to Confirm Meaning* Point to *door* and ask children how they can figure out this word. Elicit or explain that they have to do two things: look at the letters in the word, and make sure the word makes sense with *My* and the picture.

Page 10 **FOCUS STRATEGY** *Look for Word Bits and Parts* Focus on *bedroom*. Ask: **Do you see a part you know? Do you know a word that starts with those letters?**

Monitor Comprehension

1. **Where does the cat go? List the places in order. Look back at the story to check.** (*along the fence, through the gate, through the door, to the bathroom, bedroom, cupboard, bed*) **INFERENTIAL: SEQUENCE**

2. **What does the cat do at the end of the book?** (*Possible response: It curls up on the child's bed and goes to sleep.*) **INFERENTIAL: SUMMARIZE**

3. **Who is telling the story? How do you know?** (*Possible response: The child is talking, because the words say* my *book,* my *cupboard, and so on, and these things belong to the child.*) **CRITICAL: INTERPRET TEXT STRUCTURE**

Write in Response to Reading

Have groups of children draw and label pictures that lead a reader through the school and its neighborhood.

A Day at School

by Kevin Terry

Summary

A word names something associated with a day at school: *reading, computers, counting, lunch, recess, writing, school bus.* A photograph shows children engaged in an activity related to the word.

Introduce the Book

ACCESS PRIOR KNOWLEDGE Discuss the cover. Ask where the bus is most likely taking the children. Ask if children can read any words in the title. Read aloud the title; then have children read it with you. Ask children what they do during a day at school. Read to see if activities they name are in the book. **SET PURPOSE**

Guided Reading

Pages 1–2 **FOCUS STRATEGY** *Use Picture Clues to Confirm Meaning* Use prompts to help children with the word *reading:* **You said ____. Check the picture. What are the children doing?**

Pages 5–6 **FOCUS STRATEGY** *Self-Correct* Ask what the children are doing in this picture. If your children say *math,* ask what they do in math; elicit *counting.* How do they know the word on this page is not *math*? Discuss word/picture match. Explain that good readers check, then correct if they need to.

Page 14 **FOCUS STRATEGY** *Sequence Events/Summarize* Ask children to think about what the students in the book do at school. Invite volunteers to retell the events in sequential order.

Monitor Comprehension

1. **How is your school day like the one in the story? How is it different?** *(Responses will vary.)* **INFERENTIAL: MAKE COMPARISONS**

2. **Who are the adults on pages 2 and 5? How do you know?** *(Possible responses: teachers, helpers)* **INFERENTIAL: USE PICTURE CLUES/DRAW CONCLUSIONS**

3. **What is the author trying to tell you?** *(Possible responses: what school is like and what children learn in school)* **CRITICAL: RECOGNIZE AUTHOR'S PURPOSE**

Write in Response to Reading

Have children make a book about a day in your classroom. Each child can illustrate an activity and write or dictate a word or sentence to describe it.

VOCABULARY LIST
Mom
Dad
Sister
Brother
Birdie
Home

At Home
by Dean Turner

Summary

A word names a person or thing associated with home: *Mom, Dad, Sister, Brother, Birdie, Home, Me.* A photograph illustrates the word.

Introduce the Book

PREPARE TO READ Display the cover and read aloud the title. Invite children to tell whether their homes look like this one. Suggest that a home can be any place a family lives. Turn to the title page and show the camera. Explain that the pictures in the book are photographs. Have children predict who they will see in the pictures and read to find out. **PREDICT/SET PURPOSE**

Guided Reading

Page 2 **FOCUS STRATEGY** *Look for Words You Know* Focus on *Mom.* Ask: **Do you know a word that looks like this? What do you know that might help?**

Page 8 **FOCUS STRATEGY** *Look for Word Bits and Parts* Ask children who this person is. *(Brother)* How do they know he is *Brother* and not *baby*? *(The print says* B-r-o-t-h-e-r, brother.*)* Tell children they need to read carefully to be sure they read the word the author used.

Page 9 **FOCUS STRATEGY** *Make Inferences* Ask children why the bird is in this book. *(It is a pet, part of the family.)* Ask how they know this. Elicit or explain that they use clues in the book and personal experience to understand what the author does not tell them. This is called making inferences.

Monitor Comprehension

1. **Who is on the last page of the book?** *(Possible responses: "Me," another sister, the person [character] telling the story)* **INFERENTIAL: DRAW CONCLUSIONS**

2. **Why is she holding a camera?** *(Possible response: She used the camera to take photographs of her family for the book.)* **INFERENTIAL: SYNTHESIZE**

3. **What does the author think is important about a home?** *(Possible response: family members; pets; a place to be together, to have fun, to be yourself)* **CRITICAL: INTERPRET AUTHOR'S VIEWPOINT**

Write in Response to Reading

Have children make their own "At Home" books. Have them write or dictate captions for their pictures.

VOCABULARY
LIST

dogs

cats

birds

fish

hamsters

frogs

The Pet Store

by James Howard

Summary

Inviting illustrations help beginning readers read numerals and words as they count animals: 2 dogs, 3 cats, and so on, up through 7 frogs. The last page shows people in front of a pet store and repeats the title *The pet store.*

Introduce the Book

CONNECT TO EXPERIENCE Show the cover and read the title. Ask children what a pet store is, if they have ever been in one, and what it was like. Help them identify animals on the cover. *(dog, cat, fish, hamster)* Ask children what other animals they might see in a pet store. Have them read to find out what animals are in the pet store in this book. **SET PURPOSE**

Guided Reading

Page 2 **FOCUS STRATEGY** *Use Picture Clues to Confirm Meaning* Point to *dogs* and note the *d.* Point out that a pet store might have several things that begin with *d: ducks* and *doors,* for example. Have children suppose they only know the first letter of this word. How could they decide whether the word is *ducks, doors,* or *dogs*? *(Use picture clues to figure out the word.)*

Page 10 **FOCUS STRATEGY** *Look for Word Bits and Parts* Suggest that the animals in the picture might be gerbils or hamsters, unless a reader knows the difference. Ask how a reader can be sure what they are. Elicit or explain that the reader must look at the parts of the word: for example, the initial *h,* and the word part *ham.*

Pages 13–14 **FOCUS STRATEGY** *Make Inferences* Note that the author doesn't write about the people on this page. Have children use the text and personal experience to make inferences, or guesses, about what the people are doing.

Monitor Comprehension

1. **What pets are in this pet store? Reread to be sure you remember them all.** *(dogs, cats, birds, fish, hamsters, frogs; may include the parrot and rabbits on pages 13–14)* **INFERENTIAL: SUMMARIZE/IMPORTANT DETAILS**

2. **What is your favorite pet in the book? Why?** *(Possible responses: dogs, because I love dogs; frogs, because the picture is funny; the parrot, because it's the most unusual)* **CRITICAL: EXPRESS PERSONAL OPINIONS**

3. **How does the author help you read this book?** *(Possible response: He puts only one number and one word on each page, except the last, which repeats the title; uses big print; and matches text with pictures.)* **INFERENTIAL: AUTHOR'S CRAFT**

Write in Response to Reading

Have children write and illustrate a number book using favorite animals, toys, foods, and so on. They might work alone or collaborate on a shared book.

Have You Seen My Cat?

by Eric Carle

Summary

A boy searches for his lost cat. As he looks all over the world, he sees many kinds of cats before he finds his.

Introduce the Book

PREPARE TO READ Read the title, pointing to each word. Talk about the question mark. Have children predict what the book will be about. Show the page with pictures of all kinds of cats. Ask how many children can name. As you preview the pictures with children, ask: **What do you think the boy says to the people he meets? What does he find?** Have children read to find out if the boy finds his cat. **SET PURPOSE**

Guided Reading

Page 2   **FOCUS STRATEGY** *Look for Word Bits and Parts* Focus on *this.* Ask: **What part of this word do you know? Do you know a word that begins like this one?**

Page 2   **FOCUS STRATEGY** *Use Picture Clues to Confirm Meaning* Ask: **Why does the boy say, "This is not my cat?" How do you know?** (*The picture shows a lion, not a pet cat.*) Explain that readers have to use the pictures to understand what is happening on each page in this story.

Page 17   **FOCUS STRATEGY** *Make and Confirm Predictions* Ask: **Do you think the boy will ever find his cat? Where do you think the cat is?** Have children read on to check their predictions.

Monitor Comprehension

1. **Where does the boy look for his cat? Where does he finally find it?** (*Possible response: He goes around the world, looking in different places like Mexico, the desert, and India. He finally finds his cat close to home.*) **INFERENTIAL: SUMMARIZE/USE PICTURE CLUES**

2. **What are some of the cats the boy sees while he is looking for his cat?** (*Possible responses: lion, bobcat, puma, jaguar, panther, tiger, cheetah, Persian cat*) **INFERENTIAL: IMPORTANT DETAILS/USE PICTURE CLUES**

3. **What do you like about this book?** (*Possible response: I like Eric Carle's pictures; the story is pretty easy to read; I like the places the boy goes and the wild cats he sees.*) **CRITICAL: EXPRESS PERSONAL OPINIONS**

Write in Response to Reading

Have children complete the question: Have you seen my _____?
Have them illustrate the sentence. They might show where the item is hidden on one side, and where the item is found on the other.

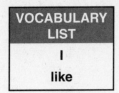

I Like Food

by Lisa Davis

Summary

A single sentence names a food enjoyed by a child, and photographs show the food and the child. On the final pages, a picture shows each child's country of origin.

Introduce the Book

PREPARE TO READ Show the cover and read the title aloud. Explain that the children on the cover live in different countries and that the book is about foods that those children like. Invite children to name foods in the background. Ask how many they have tried. Tell them that the title words and food names will be used in the story. They can read to find out what foods people like.
SET PURPOSE

Guided Reading

Pages 3–4 **FOCUS STRATEGY** *Look for Words You Know* Have children frame the word *rice*. Ask: **Do you know a word that looks like this? What do you know that might help?**

Pages 5–6 **FOCUS STRATEGY** *Look for Word Bits and Parts* Focus on the word *soup*. Ask: **Do you know a word that starts with that letter? Look at the picture. Think about the sentence.** Have children read the word.

Pages 7–8 **FOCUS STRATEGY** *Use Picture Clues to Confirm Meaning* Use prompts to guide children in reading *bread*: **You said _____. Check the picture. Does that make sense? What food do you see?**

Monitor Comprehension

1. **Who is talking in this book? How do you know?** *(Possible response: The children are talking; each uses the word* I.*)* **INFERENTIAL: DRAW CONCLUSIONS**

2. **How are the children alike? How are they different?** *(Possible response: They all like food, but they like different foods. They live in different countries.)* **INFERENTIAL: COMPARE AND CONTRAST**

3. **What foods do the children like? Which of the foods do you like? Which ones don't you like?** *(The children like pizza, rice, soup, bread, fish, pancakes; accept all reasonable responses.)* **CRITICAL: IDENTIFY WITH CHARACTERS/PERSONAL RESPONSE**

Write in Response to Reading

Have children draw their favorite food and write about it. You might brainstorm examples, such as *I like round, sweet, crunchy red apples.*

We Are Friends

by Kristi T. Butler

Summary

Simple sentences accompany pictures of children engaged in various activities. The last line repeats the title: *We are friends.*

Introduce the Book

PREPARE TO READ Show the cover and help children read the title. Ask: **How do we know the children on the cover are friends? What else do friends do together?** Preview the pictures with children and invite them to describe what the children in each picture are doing. Then have them read to find out what the friends do together. **SET PURPOSE**

Guided Reading

Page 2 **FOCUS STRATEGY** *Self-Correct* Read the text aloud, substituting *look* for *like*. Incorporating children's comments, model the strategy of self-correction; for example, "Wait—that doesn't make sense. People don't *look* running. What about *like*? *Like* makes sense, and the letters fit, too." Explain that readers must self-correct if what they read does not make sense.

Page 13 **FOCUS STRATEGY** *Make Inferences* Ask: **How does this picture show that the children are friends?** (*Possible response: They are holding hands and smiling.*) Explain that sometimes readers have to put what they read together with what they know to make inferences about the story.

Monitor Comprehension

1. **What activities do the children in this book enjoy? Look back to list them all.** (*Possible response: They like running, jumping, drawing, reading, swimming, riding bikes.*) **INFERENTIAL: SUMMARIZE**

2. **What does this book tell you about friends?** (*Possible response: Friends like to do things together; friends like at least some of the same things.*) **INFERENTIAL: DETERMINE THEME**

3. **What activities in the book do you enjoy doing with your friends? What are some other activities you and your friends enjoy?** (*Responses will vary.*) **CRITICAL: EXPRESS PERSONAL OPINIONS**

Write in Response to Reading

Have children draw and write about something they enjoy doing with friends. They can use this sentence starter or write their own: We like ____.

Five Little Ducks

by Raffi

Summary

Five little ducks go out to play, and each time Mother Duck calls, one fewer duckling returns, until none come back. Mother Duck sets out to find them, and this time, when she calls, all five come back—with families of their own!

Introduce the Book

PREVIEW Show the cover and read the title aloud. Have children count the little ducks. Read pages 1–5. Tell children this book is a song with pictures and ask if any children know the song. Point out lines that will repeat. As you look at several more pages, invite children to count the little ducks and tell what is happening in each picture. Ask: **Will the little ducks ever come back?** Read to find out, inviting children to join in on predictable lines. **SET PURPOSE**

Guided Reading

Page 1 **FOCUS STRATEGY** *Create Mental Images* Have children close their eyes and make pictures in their minds as you read page 1. Ask: **What do the ducks look like? What are they doing? What sights and sounds are in the setting?** Turn the page and compare: **How far do the ducklings really go?**

Page 2 **FOCUS STRATEGY** *Look for Word Bits and Parts* Focus on the second line. Ask: **How many times does Mother Duck say "Quack"?** Remind children that in English, the letter *q* is always followed by *u*, to make the sound /kw/.

Pages 22–23 **FOCUS STRATEGY** *Make Inferences* Remind children that sometimes readers have to make inferences, or guesses based on what they know, to decide what is happening in a story. Ask: **How long does Mother Duck wait? How does she feel? How do you know?** Read page 24 to confirm.

Monitor Comprehension

1. **How does Mother Duck find her little ducks?** *(She goes "over the hills and far away," too, and calls them.)* **INFERENTIAL: DRAW CONCLUSIONS**

2. **How do you know what happened to the little ducks?** *(Possible response: By looking at the pictures, you can tell they grew up and had families of their own.)* **METACOGNITIVE: SYNTHESIZE**

3. **What does this book (song) help readers learn?** *(Possible response: how to count backward from five)* **CRITICAL: INTERPRET TEXT STRUCTURE**

Write in Response to Reading

Have children write their own counting song, working alone or as a group:

Five little _____ went out one day, Over the _____ and far away.
_____ _____ said, "_____, _____, _____, _____," But . . . .

Happy Birthday

by Tami Butler

Summary

Duck and Pig share a birthday. Duck opens a gift from Pig; it's a hat that's too big. Pig opens a gift from Duck; it's a hat that's too small. What can they do? They swap hats! Now they can dance and have fun.

Introduce the Book

PICTURE WALK Show the cover. Have children read the title, identify the characters *(Pig and Duck)*, and talk about birthday activities they enjoy. Begin a picture walk, guiding children to note the birthday details in each picture. Note that Duck and Pig share a birthday. Invite children to read to find out what the story says about Duck and Pig's birthday. **PREVIEW/SET PURPOSE**

Guided Reading

Page 5 **FOCUS STRATEGY** *Look for Word Bits and Parts* Have a volunteer read the last word. *(today)* Ask how *today* and *birthday* are alike. *(Both include the word* day.*)* Explain that looking for word parts helps readers read new words.

Page 11 **FOCUS STRATEGY** *Use Picture Clues to Confirm Meaning* Ask: **What has happened—why do Duck and Pig need to do something?** Then read page 12, and ask: **Why are they happy again? How can you tell what has happened?** *(You can use picture clues to fill in what the text doesn't tell.)*

Page 14 **FOCUS STRATEGY** *Reread Aloud* Use prompts to guide children in reading *wow:* **You read** *now* **on the last page. What would it be if I changed the** *n* **to** *w***?**

Monitor Comprehension

1. **How do you know it is a special day for Pig and Duck?** *(Possible responses: "Happy Birthday" repeats in the title and text; the illustrations show a cake, a birthday card, and smiles.)* **INFERENTIAL: MAIN IDEA**

2. **What do Duck and Pig do on their birthday? Name the events in order.** *(Possible response: Duck mails a card; Pig makes a cake; Duck goes to Pig's house; they exchange gifts; Pig's hat is too small and Duck's is too big, so they swap; they dance together.)* **INFERENTIAL: SEQUENCE**

3. **Is this story fact or fiction? How do you know?** *(Possible response: Fiction; the animals are make-believe, and real pigs and ducks don't have birthday parties, give presents, or eat with forks.)* **CRITICAL: DISTINGUISH BETWEEN FANTASY AND REALITY**

Write in Response to Reading

Have children make a birthday card and write a message on the inside. If possible, show and discuss model birthday cards.

Five Little Monkeys Jumping on the Bed

by Eileen Christelow

Summary

Five little monkeys jump on the bed. One by one, they fall off. Each ends up with a bandaged head. Finally, they sleep, and it's the mama's turn to have fun.

Introduce the Book

PREPARE TO READ Show the cover and help children read the title. Have them use the title, the cover picture, and personal experience to guess what the book is about. Read to find out what happens to the monkeys. **CONNECT TO EXPERIENCE/SET PURPOSE**

Guided Reading

Pages 3, 4, 5 **FOCUS STRATEGY** *Use Context to Confirm Meaning* As you read aloud, pause to let children supply the last word on each page. Ask how they know the word. Elicit or explain that other words, picture clues, and experience all help them figure out the word.

Page 13 **FOCUS STRATEGY** *Make and Confirm Predictions* Ask children: **Do these monkeys look sleepy? What do you think they will do?** Prompt children to predict a repetition of previous events: jump on the bed, fall, and so on. Read on to confirm, inviting children to join in on familiar lines.

Monitor Comprehension

1. **What happens to the little monkeys?** *(Possible response: They jump on their bed. One falls off and bumps its head. The others are worried, but they forget and jump again. One by one, they all get hurt.)* **INFERENTIAL: SUMMARIZE**

2. **If you were a little monkey, would you keep jumping on the bed? Explain.** *(Responses will vary.)* **CRITICAL: IDENTIFY WITH CHARACTERS**

3. **What is the surprise at the end of the story? Why were you surprised?** *(Possible response: The mama jumps on her bed. Grown-ups don't usually jump on beds; she had told her children to stop jumping because they kept getting hurt.)* **CRITICAL: INTERPRET TEXT STRUCTURE/EXPRESS PERSONAL OPINIONS**

Write in Response to Reading

Have children write and illustrate their own countdown poem or story, working alone or in a group:

Five little _____ . . ./Four little _____ . . .

VOCABULARY
LIST

hopped
ground
pardon
tickling

"Pardon?" Said the Giraffe

by Colin West

Summary

A frog asks a giraffe what it's like up high, but the giraffe can't hear. "Pardon?" it asks. The frog climbs on other animals to reach the giraffe's nose—and falls down when the giraffe sneezes.

Introduce the Book

PREPARE TO READ Show the cover and read the title aloud. Discuss what *pardon* means. (*I didn't hear what you said. Please say it again.*) Talk about the beginning sound in *giraffe*. (*soft* g; *makes a* j *sound*) Explain that in the story a frog tries to talk to a giraffe, but the giraffe can't hear the frog. Invite children to read to find out how the frog solves this problem. **SET PURPOSE**

Guided Reading

Page 1 **FOCUS STRATEGY** *Look for Word Bits and Parts* Focus on *hopped.* Ask: **Do you know a word that starts with those letters? What part do you know?**

Page 3 **FOCUS STRATEGY** *Use Picture Clues to Confirm Meaning* Use prompts to guide children in reading *lion:* **You said _____. Check the picture. Where is the frog now?**

Page 11 **FOCUS STRATEGY** *Make and Confirm Predictions* Note that the story pattern changes here. Read page 11; ask children what they think will happen next, and what clues they have. Turn the page to check their predictions.

Monitor Comprehension

1. **Why does the giraffe say "pardon"?** (*The giraffe is tall and cannot hear the frog because the frog is small and far away.*) **INFERENTIAL: CAUSE-EFFECT**

2. **How does the frog get high enough for the giraffe to hear him? Name the steps in order.** (*He climbs on the lion's back, then the hippo's, then the elephant's, and then onto the giraffe's nose.*) **INFERENTIAL: SEQUENCE**

3. **Do you like the ending? Give your reasons.** (*Responses will vary.*) **CRITICAL: EXPRESS PERSONAL OPINIONS**

Write in Response to Reading

Tell children to pretend they are the giraffe, and to write what they thought when the frog jumped onto their nose. Have them illustrate the sentence.

VOCABULARY
LIST

saw
please
along
slower
softer
lower

Sid and Sam

by Nola Buck

Summary

Sid and Sam are friends. At first, they enjoy singing together, but then Sam gets tired. When he tells Sid to stop because the song is so long, Sid hears only the words *so long* and thinks Sam is saying good-bye.

Introduce the Book

PREPARE TO READ Show the cover and have a volunteer read the title. Introduce Sid and Sam. Explain that Sid and Sam are singing. Ask children what it means to sing slower, softer, and lower. Then ask what the phrase "So long" means. (*good-bye*) Have children read to find out what happens when Sid won't stop singing. **SET PURPOSE**

Guided Reading

Pages 4–5   **FOCUS STRATEGY**   *Self-Correct* Read aloud pages 4 and 5, substituting *was* for *saw*. Let children correct you, or correct yourself. Explain that when something doesn't make sense, readers have to stop, go back, and reread correctly.

Pages 12–13   **FOCUS STRATEGY**   *Use Picture Clues to Confirm Meaning* Ask: **How does Sid sing lower? How does she sing so low?** (*She gets lower to the ground.*) **Is this what Sam means?** (*No. He wants her to sing in a lower tone.*) Point out that the pictures show what Sid is really doing.

Page 17   **FOCUS STRATEGY**   *Make and Confirm Predictions* Ask: **Do you think Sid will stop? Read on to see if you are right.**

Monitor Comprehension

1. **Why does Sam want Sid to stop singing?** (*Possible responses: He is tired of singing; he doesn't like the way Sid sings; he wants to do something else.*) **INFERENTIAL: DETERMINE CHARACTERS' MOTIVATIONS**

2. **How does Sam solve his problem with Sid?** (*Sid won't stop singing, so Sam tells her "so long," and when she thinks he is saying good-bye, he leaves, saying "See you soon.")* **INFERENTIAL: SUMMARIZE**

3. **Is Sam's solution a good one? Explain why you think so.** (*Possible response: Yes. Sam gets away from the singing without hurting Sid's feelings. They will still be friends.*) **CRITICAL: MAKE JUDGMENTS**

Write in Response to Reading

Have children write a story about two friends. Tell them to think first about what problem the friends will have and how it will be solved.

VOCABULARY
LIST

yellow

woof

drink

light

tucked

curl

sleepy

puppy

Biscuit

by Alyssa Satin Capucilli

Summary

It's bedtime for Biscuit the puppy. His young owner gives Biscuit a snack, reads him a story, and performs other bedtime rituals—but Biscuit is lonely by himself. He follows his owner upstairs and falls asleep in her room.

Introduce the Book

PICTURE WALK Read the title. Have children name the letters and pronounce *Biscuit*. Ask who Biscuit is. Read pages 7–9 aloud while children look at the pictures. Ask them if they think Biscuit wants to go to sleep. Look through the book with children, asking what is happening on each page. Then have them read to find out if Biscuit goes to bed. **PREVIEW/SET PURPOSE**

Guided Reading

Page 10 **FOCUS STRATEGY** *Use Word Order and Context to Confirm Meaning* Focus on *snack*. Ask children what Biscuit wants. Help them use the picture, sentence structure, and decoding skills to figure out what Biscuit wants.

Page 21 **FOCUS STRATEGY** *Look for Word Bits and Parts* Focus on the word *tucked*. Ask children how they can figure out this word. Elicit or explain that they can divide the word into parts: the *-ed* ending and the base word *tuck*. Ask what *tucked in* means.

Page 26 **FOCUS STRATEGY** *Make Inferences* Ask: **Why does Biscuit finally fall asleep?** Encourage children to use clues from the story to explain their thinking.

Monitor Comprehension

1. **How would you describe Biscuit?** *(Possible responses: small, yellow, puppy, playful, needs attention)* **INFERENTIAL: DETERMINE CHARACTERS' TRAITS**

2. **How does the girl feel about Biscuit? How do you know?** *(Possible responses: She loves him; she likes to take care of him. She gives him snacks, water, a story, a comfy bed; she smiles when he falls asleep in her room.)* **INFERENTIAL: DETERMINE CHARACTERS' EMOTIONS**

3. **Suppose Biscuit were your dog. What would you do to get him to sleep? Why?** *(Responses will vary.)* **CRITICAL: EXPRESS PERSONAL OPINIONS**

Write in Response to Reading

Have children write and illustrate a list of at least three things they like to do before bed.

Big Brown Bear

by David McPhail

Summary

Big Brown Bear has a project: to paint the door and window shutters of a tree house. However, he runs into difficulties when Little Bear creates interruptions.

Introduce the Book

PICTURE WALK Show the cover and help children read the title to prepare for the story. Ask: **Who is this? What is he going to do? What color paint will he use? How do you know?** Have children preview pictures in the book while you ask questions that will help them read. **What does Bear look like? Where is he going? What is happening here?** Then have them read to find out if the treehouse gets painted. **PREVIEW/SET PURPOSE**

Guided Reading

Page 5 **FOCUS STRATEGY** *Look for Words You Know* Use prompts to guide children in reading *down*: **You've already read *brown*. What would it be if I changed the *br* to *d*?**

Page 8 **FOCUS STRATEGY** *Use Picture Clues to Confirm Meaning* Focus on *bat*. Prompt a child who misreads this word: **You said *ball*. Check the picture. What is Little Bear holding?**

Page 15 **FOCUS STRATEGY** *Make Predictions* Have children examine the picture on page 15 for any clues that will help them predict what might happen next.

Monitor Comprehension

1. **What happens to Big Brown Bear in the story?** *(Possible response: He tries to paint a tree house, gets hit by Little Bear's ball, falls off the ladder, gets covered with paint, and has to wash.)* **INFERENTIAL: SUMMARIZE**

2. **If the story did not stop here, what do you think would happen next?** *(Possible response: Bear would get covered with green paint, clean up, and try again to paint.)* **INFERENTIAL: SPECULATE**

3. **How are the bears in this story like real bears? How are they different?** *(Possible response: They are like real bears in that they are brown and have four paws. They are unlike real bears in that they paint, play ball, ride bikes, wear hats, work on tree houses, and show human emotions.)* **CRITICAL: DISTINGUISH BETWEEN FANTASY AND REALITY**

Write in Response to Reading

Have children write and illustrate another page to the story that tells what happens after Little Bear runs into the ladder.

Two Bear Cubs

by Ann Jonas

Summary

Two bear cubs leave the den with their mother. They encounter a skunk, outrun it, and get lost. As they meet a swarm of bees, and try to fish, they wonder where their mother is. The reader knows she is always nearby.

Introduce the Book

PREPARE TO READ   Show the cover and help children use the picture to figure out the title. Have them share what they know about bears. Ask what adventures two bear cubs might have in the wild. Preview the pictures with children. Have them read to find out what happens to the cubs in the story. **ACCESS PRIOR KNOWLEDGE/SET PURPOSE**

Guided Reading

Page 2   **FOCUS STRATEGY**   *Use Context Clues to Confirm Meaning* Use prompts to guide children in reading unfamiliar words: **Where's the tricky word? Read that sentence again and check the picture. What would make sense?** Elicit or explain that the pictures and surrounding words help readers figure out new words.

Page 7   **FOCUS STRATEGY**   *Look for Word Bits and Parts* Focus on *smell.* Ask: **Do you know a word that looks like this? Do you know a word that starts with those letters?**

Page 8   **FOCUS STRATEGY**   *Self-Correct* Children often self-correct when reading. Use prompts to bring this to a child's attention: **You said _____ . Then you changed it to _____ . How did you know?**

Monitor Comprehension

1. **What adventures do the two bear cubs have? Try to list them in order.** *(Possible response: They are chased by a skunk, find a honey tree, get chased by bees, and try to fish.)* **INFERENTIAL: SUMMARIZE/SEQUENCE**

2. **Where is the mother bear? What is she doing? How do you know?** *(She is always nearby, watching over the cubs; she is visible in the illustrations.)* **INFERENTIAL: IMPORTANT DETAILS**

3. **What do you think the cubs learn from their adventures?** *(Possible responses: to run from skunks; honey is tasty, but bees sting; fish are hard to catch; they still need their mother)* **CRITICAL: INTERPRET STORY EVENTS**

Write in Response to Reading

Have children work with partners or in small groups to write and illustrate a story about another animal mother and her babies.

Shoe Town

by Janet Stevens and Susan Stevens Crummel

Summary

A mouse looks forward to a bath and a nap now that her babies have grown up and left her house in a shoe. When her plans are interrupted by visitors from other stories, the mouse starts a whole town of shoes.

Introduce the Book

PICTURE WALK Show the cover and read the title. Ask questions to help children think about the title and picture clues: **What are the houses in *Shoe Town* made of? What would a town of shoes look like?** Have children look at the pictures and identify the characters. Read to find out how the shoe town grows. **PREVIEW/SET PURPOSE**

Guided Reading

Pages 1–2 **FOCUS STRATEGY** *Look for Word Bits and Parts* Ask: **What do you notice about the words at the end of each page?** (*They rhyme, even though the end sound is spelled differently.*) Tell children that the story is a rhyming poem. Invite them to look for rhymes and notice those that are spelled differently.

Page 9 **FOCUS STRATEGY** *Make and Confirm Predictions* Before reading page 10, ask: **Will the mouse get to have her bath and her nap? What do you think will happen?** Prompt children to predict repetition. (*Other animals will come and ask for room. Mouse will say her shoe is too little. She will tell them to look for shoes of their own.*) Read to confirm predictions.

Page 22 **FOCUS STRATEGY** *Reread Aloud* Use prompts to help children read unfamiliar words: **Where's the tricky word? Look at the beginning. Look at the end. Read that sentence again. Try your word.**

Monitor Comprehension

1. **Why does the mouse want a bath and a nap?** (*Possible response: She worked hard to raise her babies, and wants to relax and rest now that they're gone.*) **INFERENTIAL: DETERMINE CHARACTERS' MOTIVATIONS**

2. **How does Shoe Town get started?** (*Possible response: Visitors come and want to stay with the mouse. Her shoe house is too small, so she tells them to find their own shoe houses to live in nearby.*) **INFERENTIAL: SUMMARIZE**

3. **What do you like about this story?** (*Responses will vary. Children may like the rhymes, repetition, funny pictures, guest characters, or clever idea of shoe houses.*) **CRITICAL: EXPRESS PERSONAL OPINIONS**

Write in Response to Reading

Have children write and illustrate a story that begins, "If I lived in a shoe. . . ." They might write alone, or collaborate on a shared book.

Leo the Late Bloomer

by Robert Kraus

Summary

Leo the young tiger is a late bloomer. Unlike his peers, Leo can't read or write or draw. His father grows concerned, but his mother always has confidence that Leo will develop at his own pace.

Introduce the Book

PREPARE TO READ Show the cover and read the title. Ask who Leo is. Explain that the expression *late bloomer* means "someone who doesn't always keep up with others." As children look at the pictures, ask questions that will help them preview unfamiliar words. Have them read to find out what happens to Leo. **SET PURPOSE**

Guided Reading

Page 1 **FOCUS STRATEGY** *Look for Word Bits and Parts* Ask children what word is made from smaller words. Help children identify the word parts. Remind them to look for word parts when reading unfamiliar words.

Page 6 **FOCUS STRATEGY** *Use Picture Clues to Confirm Meaning* Focus on the word *sloppy*. Use prompts: **You said ____. Does that make sense? Check the picture. Look how neatly the other animals are eating, and how messy Leo is.**

Page 14 **FOCUS STRATEGY** *Make Inferences* Ask children what Leo's mother means when she says, "A watched bloomer doesn't bloom." Help them draw on context and experience to figure out what she means.

Monitor Comprehension

1. **What is Leo's problem? How is the problem solved?** *(Possible response: He is a late bloomer. He waits until he is able to do what his friends can do.)* **INFERENTIAL: SUMMARIZE**

2. **What do Leo's mother and father think about Leo?** *(Possible response: Leo's father worries that something is wrong with Leo; he wants Leo to change quickly. Leo's mother is patient and sure Leo will be fine.)* **INFERENTIAL: DETERMINE CHARACTERS' EMOTIONS**

3. **What do you think the author is trying to tell readers?** *(Possible response: People learn when they are ready. Some are "late bloomers," and need more time.)* **CRITICAL: INTERPRET THEME**

Write in Response to Reading

Have children imagine they are Leo's friend. Before Leo blooms, they notice he is sad. Ask what they could say to make him feel better. Have them write and illustrate a letter that would help Leo cheer up.

VOCABULARY LIST

heavy

engine

siren

search

straight

Fire Fighters

by Norma Simon

Summary

Illustrations show Dalmatian dogs carrying out the activities of human fire fighters. The text explains how fire fighters fight fires and rescue people. It also describes the equipment fire fighters use and their daily routines.

Introduce the Book

ACCESS PRIOR KNOWLEDGE Show the cover and read the title. Ask who the fire fighters are in this picture. Explain that the book tells what real fire fighters do, but the fire fighters in the pictures are dogs instead of people. Discuss what fire fighters do, drawing on children's prior knowledge. Have them read to learn more. **SET PURPOSE**

Guided Reading

Page 4 **FOCUS STRATEGY** *Look for Word Bits and Parts* Have children find the two words that make up the word *firehouse—fire* and *house*. Guide them in using the two small, familiar words to figure out what a *firehouse* is.

Page 11 **FOCUS STRATEGY** *Make Inferences* Point out that the story does not tell what happened to the dogs. Readers have to infer, or guess, what happened, using what they read and what they know. Ask: **What do you think happened to the dogs in the blankets? How did the fire fighters help?**

Page 22 **FOCUS STRATEGY** *Sequence Events/Summarize* Help children review what they learned from the book. Ask: **What do fire fighters do before a fire? What do they do at a fire? What do they do after a fire?**

Monitor Comprehension

1. **Why must there always be some fire fighters at the firehouse?** *(Possible response: A fire can happen at any time, so fire fighters have to be ready.)* **INFERENTIAL: DRAW CONCLUSIONS**

2. **What qualities do you think a person needs to be a fire fighter? Give reasons for your answer.** *(Possible response: A fire fighter needs to be brave because fires are dangerous; strong because the equipment is heavy; and smart to figure out how the fire started.)* **INFERENTIAL: SYNTHESIZE**

3. **After reading this book, would you like to be a fire fighter? Why or why not?** *(Possible response: Yes; fire fighting is an exciting and important job. I'd like to drive a fire truck.)* **CRITICAL: EXPRESS PERSONAL OPINIONS**

Write in Response to Reading

Have children choose a job they know something about, and write and illustrate their own books about *My Day as a* _____.

Ask Mr. Bear

by Marjorie Flack

Summary

Danny wants to give his mother a special birthday gift. He asks his animal friends, but each offers something Danny's mother already has. Finally, Mr. Bear suggests the perfect gift, a birthday bear hug.

Introduce the Book

PICTURE WALK Read aloud the title, pointing to each word. Explain that the boy, Danny, wants to give his mother a birthday gift, and his animal friends try to help. Turn to page 1 and talk about the use of quotation marks. Then walk through the book, inviting children to name each new animal. Invite children to predict who will give Danny the best idea. **PREDICT/SET PURPOSE**

Guided Reading

Page 2   **FOCUS STRATEGY**   *Make and Confirm Predictions* Ask children what they think Mrs. Hen could give Danny. Then have them listen to the next page to confirm their predictions. You can do this each time Danny asks his question.

Page 3   **FOCUS STRATEGY**   *Look for Words You Know* Use prompts to help children read *cluck:* **You know *duck*. What would it be if I changed the *d* to *cl*?**

Page 13   **FOCUS STRATEGY**   *Use Picture Clues to Confirm Meaning* Ask children what the word *galloped* means. Note that the picture shows Danny and the animals running—or "galloping."

Monitor Comprehension

1. **Why doesn't Danny want the gifts the farm animals offer him?** *(His mother already has the things they offer, and he wants to give her something she doesn't already have.)* **INFERENTIAL: CAUSE-EFFECT**

2. **What secret does Mr. Bear tell Danny? How do you know?** *(He tells Danny to give his mother a big birthday bear hug. I know because Danny runs home and gives his mother a hug.)* **INFERENTIAL: DRAW CONCLUSIONS**

3. **Why is a hug just the right gift for Danny's mother?** *(Possible responses: It is something Danny can give all by himself. It is a gift only he can give, and it shows how much he loves her.)* **CRITICAL: MAKE JUDGMENTS**

Write in Response to Reading

Have children write coupons for something they could give to someone they love. You might provide a sample coupon for them to copy and fill in.

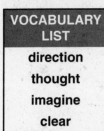

VOCABULARY LIST

direction

thought

imagine

clear

The Big Dipper

by Franklyn M. Branley

Summary

A girl shares her knowledge of the stars, including information about the Big Dipper, the North Star, and the Little Dipper.

Introduce the Book

PREPARE TO READ Show the cover and read the title. Explain that the Big Dipper is the constellation in the picture, and that the girl on the cover will tell them about it. Ask children if they have ever looked at the stars. Record what they know about the Big Dipper. Suggest that as they read, children look for information to add to their list. **SET PURPOSE**

Guided Reading

Page 13 **FOCUS STRATEGY** *Look for Word Bits and Parts* Focus on the word *handle*. Ask: **Do you know a word that starts with those letters? Do you think it looks like ____ ?**

Page 16 **FOCUS STRATEGY** *Create Mental Images* Invite children to close their eyes and picture in their minds how the Big Dipper looks on a summer night, then on a winter night.

Page 24 **FOCUS STRATEGY** *Use Context Clues to Confirm Meaning* After reading, ask children what *Ursa Major* means. Have them find clues in the text that tell what it means.

Monitor Comprehension

1. **Tell at least three things you learned about the Big Dipper by reading this book.** *(Possible responses: The Big Dipper looks different in summer and winter. There are seven stars in the Big Dipper. The Big Dipper is always found in the north part of the sky. The Big Dipper is part of Ursa Major.)* **INFERENTIAL: SUMMARIZE**

2. **Read pages 19 and 22 again. How can you find the Little Dipper?** *(Use the Big Dipper's bowl stars to point to the North Star, which is part of the Little Dipper's handle.)* **INFERENTIAL: SYNTHESIZE**

3. **Why are the pictures important in this book?** *(Possible response: The pictures show what the girl is telling about. They let you see what the Big Dipper and Ursa Major look like.)* **CRITICAL: INTERPRET TEXT STRUCTURE**

Write in Response to Reading

Have children write a day and night book. They can draw things they see in the sky during the day and at night, and write sentences about their pictures.

Little Fox Goes to the End of the World

by Ann Tompert

Summary

For her mother, who is a patient and loving listener, an imaginative little fox spins a tale of worldwide adventures that she plans to undertake.

Introduce the Book

PREPARE TO READ Show the cover and read the title. Ask children who is on the cover and what they think she is going to do. Preview the illustrations. Elicit or explain that Little Fox is telling her mother about imaginary travels. Suggest that children read to find out where she pretends to go. **PREVIEW/SET PURPOSE**

Guided Reading

Page 1 **FOCUS STRATEGY** *Use Picture Clues to Confirm Meaning* As you read aloud page 1, pause and let children use picture clues to supply the word *butterfly*. Pause again to ask what Mother Fox is doing. Remind children that they can often use the pictures to figure out words.

Page 7 **FOCUS STRATEGY** *Reread Aloud* Use prompts to help children read unfamiliar words: **Why did you stop? What do you think the word is? Look at the beginning. Read that sentence again. Think about what would make sense. Try your word.**

Monitor Comprehension

1. **What places does Little Fox visit on her imaginary trip to the end of the world?** *(forest, mountains, desert, river, sea, island of the One-eyed Cats)* **INFERENTIAL: SUMMARIZE**

2. **What words would you use to describe Little Fox? What words would you use to describe her mother?** *(Possible responses: Little Fox is imaginative, a good storyteller, brave, funny. Her mother is a good listener, nice, patient, encouraging.)* **INFERENTIAL: DETERMINE CHARACTERS' TRAITS**

3. **How do you know that Little Fox is only pretending to go places?** *(Possible response: She is always talking to her mother at home.)* **CRITICAL: DISTINGUISH BETWEEN FANTASY AND REALITY**

Write in Response to Reading

Have children write an ending for this sentence starter: *I would like to be with Little Fox when _____.* Have them illustrate the scene they write about.

Peeping and Sleeping

by Fran Manushkin

Summary

When Barry hears a peeping sound in the night, his father takes him to the pond to learn about the tiny frogs called *spring peepers*. Back home, Barry finds a peeper in his slipper. He sets it free and soon falls asleep.

Introduce the Book

ACCESS PRIOR KNOWLEDGE Read the title. Let children make peeping noises. Ask what the cover picture shows. Explain that the story is about a boy named Barry. When he hears a peeping sound in the night, his father takes him outside to see what is making the sound. Invite children to describe what they have seen and heard when they have been outside at night. Have them predict what is making the peeping sound in this story. Read to find out. **PREDICT/SET PURPOSE**

Guided Reading

Pages 5–8 **FOCUS STRATEGY** *Create Mental Images* Have children close their eyes and imagine they are Barry as you read or reread pages 5–8. Tell them to keep their eyes closed as they tell you what they see, hear, and feel.

Page 14 **FOCUS STRATEGY** *Look for Words You Know* Use prompts to help children read *deep*: **Do you know a word that looks like this? You know *peep*. What would it be if I changed the *p* to *d*?**

Page 24 **FOCUS STRATEGY** *Use Picture Clues to Confirm Meaning* Have children use the picture to help them understand the text. Ask: **What are Barry and his dad doing? What does Barry mean when he says "Here's our pond"?**

Monitor Comprehension

1. **How do Barry and his father feel about each other? How do you know?** (*Possible response: They love each other. Barry's dad takes care of him, takes him to see the peepers, and pretends with him. Barry trusts his dad; he goes with him even when he is a little afraid of the dark.*) **INFERENTIAL: DETERMINE CHARACTERS' EMOTIONS**

2. **What facts does this book tell you about peepers?** (*Peepers come out in the spring. They live near ponds. They peep at night. They can find their way back to a pond.*) **INFERENTIAL: SUMMARIZE**

3. **Why is *Peeping and Sleeping* a good title for this book?** (*Possible responses: The little frogs are peeping all night, and Barry and his dad are sleeping.*) **CRITICAL: AUTHOR'S CRAFT/APPRECIATE LANGUAGE**

Write in Response to Reading

Have children draw night pictures and label animals that make sounds in the night, including insects, pond creatures, and birds.

Leon and Bob

by Simon James

Summary

Leon's imaginary friend, Bob, keeps him company in his new home. One day a boy moves in next door. Leon works up the courage to introduce himself and make a new friend—whose name also happens to be Bob.

Introduce the Book

PREPARE TO READ Show the cover and read the title. Explain that Leon is reading a letter to Bob, who is sitting in the chair. Ask children who they think Bob is. Have children preview the pictures on pages 2–8 and discuss what Leon and Bob are doing. Ask what happens on page 10. Invite children to predict what will happen and read to find out. **PREDICT/SET PURPOSE**

Guided Reading

Pages 4, 6, 8 **FOCUS STRATEGY** *Create Mental Images* Have children create a mental picture of where Bob is and what he is doing in each illustration.

Page 9 **FOCUS STRATEGY** *Self-Correct* Use prompts to reinforce a child's use of this strategy: **You said _____. Then you changed it to _____. How did you know?** Explain that good readers self-correct if what they read does not make sense.

Page 17 **FOCUS STRATEGY** *Make Inferences* Tell children that the author doesn't answer the question on this page; they have to answer it themselves. Guide them in using story clues and their own thinking to decide why Bob isn't there.

Monitor Comprehension

1. **Why does Leon create an imaginary friend? Explain your thinking.** *(Possible response: He is lonely because he is new in town. He misses his dad and wants someone to talk to. He wants a friend to share things with.)* **INFERENTIAL: CAUSE-EFFECT/DETERMINE CHARACTERS' EMOTIONS**

2. **Do you think Leon and the real Bob will be good friends? Tell why or why not.** *(Possible response: Yes. They are both new in town and friendly. They both like soccer.)* **CRITICAL: EXPRESS PERSONAL OPINIONS**

3. **Why is *Leon and Bob* a good title for this story?** *(Leon is the main character. His imaginary friend and his real friend are both named Bob.)* **INFERENTIAL: AUTHOR'S CRAFT**

Write in Response to Reading

Have children draw and write about a friend, real or imaginary. Help them brainstorm and list ideas to include, such as name, age, qualities, and interests.

The Art Lesson

by Tomie dePaola

Summary

Tommy wants to be an artist, and he is frustrated by his art class in school. Finally, he and the teacher compromise: after Tommy copies the class drawing, he can make his own picture with his own crayons.

Introduce the Book

PREVIEW Display the book cover and read the title. Explain that the main character's name is Tommy, and the story is based on experiences from the author's life. Read the dedication page and ask what it tells about the author. Suggest that children read to find out what happens in Tommy's art lesson. **SET PURPOSE**

Guided Reading

Page 8 **FOCUS STRATEGY** *Use Picture Clues to Confirm Meaning* Use prompts to help children read *grocery*: **Check the picture. What would make sense? What kind of store is this?** Explain that good readers use picture clues to help them read.

Page 13 **FOCUS STRATEGY** *Reread Aloud* To guide children in reading *kindergarten*, prompt them with: **Where's the tricky word? Look at the beginning. What do you see? Read that sentence again. Think about what would make sense. Try your word.**

Page 25 **FOCUS STRATEGY** *Make and Confirm Predictions* Ask children what they think will happen next. Then have them read to find out.

Monitor Comprehension

1. **How can you tell Tommy wants to be an artist?** *(Possible response: He practices constantly, wants to learn, and tries not to copy.)* **METACOGNITIVE: DETERMINE CHARACTERS' TRAITS**

2. **What happens in Tommy's art lesson?** *(Possible response: He doesn't want to draw the Pilgrims because "real artists don't copy." Finally, he and the teacher agree that he will draw the Pilgrims first and then draw his own picture.)* **INFERENTIAL: SUMMARIZE**

3. **If you were Tommy, what would you do when the art teacher told you to copy the picture she drew? Tell why.** *(Responses will vary.)* **CRITICAL: IDENTIFY WITH CHARACTERS/EXPRESS PERSONAL OPINIONS**

Write in Response to Reading

Have children use crayons to make a palette of their favorite colors on a piece of paper. Then have them label the colors on their palette.

Four Fur Feet

by Margaret Wise Brown

Summary

In this whimsical ballad, a creature with four furry feet travels around the world, seeing boats, trains, and animals. Then he curls up on the grass and takes a nap. In his dreams, he begins his walk around the world again.

Introduce the Book

PREVIEW AND PREDICT Read aloud the title, pointing to each word. Ask children to look at the cover and predict what the book will be about. Read aloud the first three pages. Ask children what they notice about the story. *(It is a poem. It has rhythm like a song. Lines repeat. The last line ends in –O.)* Invite children to read with you as the pattern becomes familiar. **SET PURPOSE**

Guided Reading

Page 2 **FOCUS STRATEGY** *Look for Words You Know* To help children read unfamiliar words, have them think about words they know. Ask: **Do you know a word that looks like this? What do you know that might help?**

Pages 5–6 **FOCUS STRATEGY** *Use Picture Clues/Make Inferences* Ask children what time of day it is as the creature is walking. Ask how they know it's nighttime. Invite them to note changes in time as the story continues.

Page 21, **FOCUS STRATEGY** *Sequence Events/Summarize* Explain that to *summarize* means to tell the main events of a story in the order that they happened. Help children summarize the story. Ask what happens first, next, and last.

Monitor Comprehension

1. **What is this creature like?** *(Responses will vary.)* **INFERENTIAL: DETERMINE CHARACTERS' TRAITS**

2. **How is the end of the story like the beginning? How is it different?** *(Possible response: The words are the same; the creature is walking around the world again, but this time it is dreaming.)* **INFERENTIAL: COMPARE AND CONTRAST**

3. **Why do you think the author wrote this story as a poem?** *(Possible responses: to make the story fun to read; to help people practice reading and learn new words)* **CRITICAL: RECOGNIZE AUTHOR'S PURPOSE**

Write in Response to Reading

Have children work alone or with partners to write rhymes about fun places to visit. They might use a rhyme from the story as a model.

Man On The Moon

by Anastasia Suen

Summary

This is an account of the first moon landing. Text and pictures take readers back to 1969 to share the amazing journey of astronauts Armstrong, Aldrin, and Collins.

Introduce the Book

PICTURE WALK Show the cover and read the title. Ask children what they see in the picture. Explain that this book tells about the very first time people walked on the moon. Have children look at the illustrations and describe what is happening. Have them read the selection to learn more. **PREVIEW/SET PURPOSE**

Guided Reading

Page 1 **FOCUS STRATEGY** *Look for Word Bits and Parts* Focus on the word *visitors*. Ask: **Do you see a part you know?** *(is, it, or)* Remind children to look for parts they know when reading unfamiliar words.

Page 7 **FOCUS STRATEGY** *Create Mental Images* Have children shut their eyes and picture in their minds what the astronauts were doing, thinking, and feeling during their trip through space. Invite children to share their ideas.

Monitor Comprehension

1. **What happened between the time the spacecraft left Earth and the time the *Eagle* landed on the moon?** *(Possible response: The rockets dropped off; the astronauts headed for the moon in the capsule; when they got near the moon, they looked for a place to land; Aldrin and Armstrong moved into the Eagle; then the Eagle landed on the moon.)* **INFERENTIAL: SEQUENCE**

2. **What did Neil Armstrong say when he stepped on the moon?** *("That's one small step for man, one giant leap for mankind.")* **INFERENTIAL: USE TEXT STRUCTURE**

3. **Would you want to be an astronaut? Why or why not?** *(Possible responses: Yes; it would be exciting and challenging. No; it would be dangerous and I might not get home.)* **CRITICAL: EXPRESS PERSONAL OPINIONS**

Write in Response to Reading

Have children choose different events in the selection to write about and illustrate. Bind their pages to make a class book, *The First Trip to the Moon*.

Henry and Mudge and the Happy Cat

by Cynthia Rylant

Summary

Henry and his dog Mudge find a cat on their doorstep. The cat stays until Henry's family finds its owner, a nice policeman.

Introduce the Book

PREPARE TO READ Show the cover and read the title. Help children guess who the cover characters are. Lead a picture walk through the book, introducing vocabulary that may be unfamiliar to children. Suggest that they read to find out what happens to the cat. **PREVIEW/SET PURPOSE**

Guided Reading

Page 8 **FOCUS STRATEGY** *Use Picture Clues to Confirm Meaning* Have a volunteer read aloud the description of the cat. Have other children tell how the picture helps them understand the description. Remind children that pictures can help them figure out new words.

Pages 10–11 **FOCUS STRATEGY** *Make Inferences* Ask: **How does Henry feel about the cat? How does Mudge feel? How does Henry's father feel?** Guide children in using text clues and personal experience to make inferences, or good guesses, about characters' emotions. *(Example: Tail-wagging means Mudge is happy.)*

Monitor Comprehension

1. **What happens to the shabby cat in chapter two? How does it change?** *(Possible response: In one week it turns from shabby to happy, makes itself at home, and becomes Mudge's mother.)* **INFERENTIAL: SUMMARIZE/USE TEXT STRUCTURE**

2. **Why do Henry and his family make posters? Do the posters work?** *(They make posters to find the cat's owner. Yes—the policeman comes to claim Dave.)* **INFERENTIAL: CAUSE-EFFECT**

3. **Do you think Henry's family did the right thing with the cat? What would you have done? Tell why.** *(Responses will vary.)* **CRITICAL: EXPRESS PERSONAL OPINIONS**

Write in Response to Reading

Have children make a poster that would help Henry's family find the cat's owner.

VOCABULARY LIST

wheat

pole

soil

sprinkle

root

pale

shoots

How a Seed Grows

by Helene J. Jordan

Summary

In this work of nonfiction, the writer describes what seeds are and how they grow. Children can follow the step-by-step directions to observe firsthand the changes that take place as a seed grows.

Introduce the Book

CONNECT TO EXPERIENCE Show the cover and read the title. Have children look at the cover picture and tell what the girl is doing. Ask children what they know about seeds. Record their ideas in a K-W-L chart. Then ask what they want to know and record their responses. Suggest that children read to learn more about how seeds grow. **SET PURPOSE**

Guided Reading

Page 6 **FOCUS STRATEGY** *Look for Word Bits and Parts* Write *grandmother* and *grandfather*. Ask: **What small words make up these long words?** Remind children to look for parts they know in long words.

Page 9 **FOCUS STRATEGY** *Use Context Clues to Confirm Meaning* Point out the word *containers*. Ask: **How can you figure out what *containers* are?** Guide children in recognizing that they can use the preceding sentence and the picture to understand what the word means.

Page 23 **FOCUS STRATEGY** *Create Mental Images* Have children close their eyes and picture a bean seed beginning to grow. Ask: **What are the *root hairs*? What is the *shoot*? How do the words *hair* and *shoot* help you see what is happening to the plant?**

Monitor Comprehension

1. **What do the children do to get the seeds ready to grow?** *(Possible response: Plant and cover with a little soil; place in a sunny window; water a little every day.)* **INFERENTIAL: SUMMARIZE**

2. **Why do the children dig up the seeds they have planted?** *(Possible response: They want to see how the seeds are growing under the soil, so they dig up a seed every day or so to see what is happening.)* **INFERENTIAL: DETERMINE CHARACTERS' MOTIVATIONS**

3. **What did you learn about seeds that you did not know before reading this book?** *(Possible responses: I did not know that little roots are called root hairs; I didn't know you could plant seeds in eggshells.)* **INFERENTIAL: CLASSIFY**

Write in Response to Reading

Have children write riddles about things that grow. Give them the following example to follow: "I am orange and I grow under the ground. What am I?" *(a carrot)*

VOCABULARY LIST

sniff
chomp
slice
wander
permission
warn
salute

Listen Buddy
by Helen Lester

Summary

Buddy the bunny has trouble listening. When his parents ask him to do something, he makes mistakes. When a mistake gets him into trouble with a villain, the Scruffy Varmint, Buddy finally learns to listen.

Introduce the Book

PICTURE WALK Show the cover and read the title aloud. Explain that in this story, Buddy learns a lesson about listening. Have children look at the pictures and tell what they think will happen. Suggest that they read to find out what Buddy learns. **PREDICT/SET PURPOSE**

Guided Reading

Page 3 **FOCUS STRATEGY** *Use Context Clues to Confirm Meaning* Ask children what special feature Buddy's father has. *(a big nose)* Then point out the word *sniffer.* Guide children in using what they already know to read and understand *sniffer.*

Page 9 **FOCUS STRATEGY** *Use Picture Clues to Confirm Meaning* Have children look carefully at the illustration to tell what Buddy did when his father asked for a pen. Use the same strategy on page 11.

Page 18 **FOCUS STRATEGY** *Make and Confirm Predictions* Tell children that Buddy is going to help the Scruffy Varmint make soup. Have them predict what will happen in the rest of the story and read to see what actually happens.

Monitor Comprehension

1. **What is Buddy like at the beginning of the story?** *(Possible responses: He has big ears. He wants to help, but because he doesn't listen well, he makes a lot of mistakes.)* **INFERENTIAL: DETERMINE CHARACTERS' TRAITS**

2. **How does Buddy learn to listen?** *(Possible response: He meets the Scruffy Varmint, who gets angry when Buddy wrecks his soup. When the varmint threatens to eat "the bunnyrabbit who never listens," Buddy listens and runs away.)* **INFERENTIAL: CAUSE-EFFECT**

3. **What do you think the author is trying to tell readers?** *(Possible response: It is important to listen.)* **CRITICAL: INTERPRET THEME**

Write in Response to Reading

Have children write sentences or short poems about things they like to listen to. Have them draw pictures to illustrate their writing.

My Dog

by Hayley Novak

Summary

A little girl uses a repetitive pattern to tell the many things her dog can do, some of which she can do, too.

Introduce the Book

PICTURE WALK Tell children that this book is called *My Dog* and that it is about a little girl and her dog. Conduct a picture walk by discussing the dog's actions and any words children recognize that match the pictures (*nap, sit,* etc.). Suggest that children read the book to find out what the girl wants to tell about her dog. **PREDICT/SET PURPOSE**

Guided Reading

Page 2 **FOCUS STRATEGY** *Use Picture Clues to Confirm Meaning* Especially with this patterned text, readers can use the pictures to confirm words. Use the following prompts to coach the reading of the word *run*.

You said *jump*. Look at the word. It begins with *r*. Does *jump* begin like *rabbit*? What are the dog and the girl doing that begins with *r*?

Page 5 **FOCUS STRATEGY** *Self-Correct* Early readers using picture clues may use too many words. They will often notice when the words they say do not match the number of words in the text. Use the following prompts to support the reading of the word *bark*.

You said *bark at a cat*. Then you changed it to *bark*. How did you know to change it? I like the way you figured out that you had too many words.

Monitor Comprehension

1. **What things can the dog do that the girl can do, too?** *(run, jump, walk, nap, sit, hug)* **LITERAL: NOTE DETAILS**

2. **How do the girl and the dog feel about each other? Why do you think that?** *(Possible response: They love one another. The picture shows a heart and them hugging.)* **INFERENTIAL: DETERMINE CHARACTERS' EMOTIONS**

3. **What are some other things the girl might do with her dog?** *(Possible responses: play catch, race, swim)* **CRITICAL: SPECULATE**

Write in Response to Reading

Invite children to name pets they have or would like to have. List their responses on the board. Then have children complete the sentence *My _____ can play*. Ask children to choose a pet, draw a picture of it, and write the completed sentence under the picture. Bind children's work into a class book titled *Our Pets*.

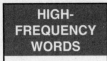
What a Shower!

by Ben Farrell

Summary

Two children and three animals play in a fire hydrant sprinkler.

Introduce the Book

PICTURE WALK Show children the title page of *What a Shower!* and discuss what is happening. Then have them look through the first seven pages to identify the characters. Discuss the characters' actions by using phrases similar to those in the text, such as *Here's a cat. It's jumping in.* Ask what kind of shower the characters will have. **PREDICT/SET PURPOSE**

Guided Reading

Page 4 **FOCUS STRATEGY** *Use Picture Clues to Confirm Meaning* Readers can use pictures to confirm words. Use the following prompts to coach the reading of the word *bird*.

You said *boy*. Look at the picture. Is the boy in the water now? What animal do you see in the water on this page?

Page 8 **FOCUS STRATEGY** *Reread Aloud* The word pattern changes on this page. Use the following prompts to guide children in reading the sentence.

Read that sentence again. Run your finger under the words as you say them. Does it look right? Think about what would make sense.

Monitor Comprehension

1. **What are two kinds of showers the characters have in this story?** *(They get a shower from the fire hydrant, and they get a shower when the dog shakes itself.)* **LITERAL: NOTE DETAILS**

2. **Why do you think the characters are splashing in the water?** *(Responses will vary.)* **CRITICAL: INTERPRET CHARACTERS' MOTIVATIONS**

3. **Which character do you think enjoys the shower most? How can you tell?** *(Responses will vary.)* **CRITICAL: DETERMINE CHARACTERS' EMOTIONS**

Write in Response to Reading

Ask children to imagine that zoo animals came to play in the fire hydrant shower. Have children brainstorm animals they might see and complete the sentence *The _____ jumps in.* Then have them illustrate their sentences. Bind the pages into a class book for children to read and share.

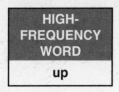

Spring Pops Up

by Meish Goldish

Summary

Children will get a surprise as they discover what might pop up in a garden in the spring.

Introduce the Book

PICTURE WALK Show children the cover as you read the title *Spring Pops Up*. Ask what this title makes them think about. Then invite children to share what they know about how gardens grow. Use the phrase *pops up* as you discuss the pictures with children. Before turning each page, have them predict what may pop up next. **PREDICT/SET PURPOSE**

Guided Reading

Page 4 **FOCUS STRATEGY** *Use Picture Clues to Confirm Meaning* Use the following prompts to support the reading of the word *flower*.

You said ____. Look at the picture. Does that make sense? What is growing from the leaf?

Page 8 **FOCUS STRATEGY** *Look for Word Bits and Parts* Readers look for letters they know when reading new words. Use the following prompts to coach the reading of the word *Lunch*.

Look at the word. It begins with *l*. The characters are having a picnic, but *picnic* does not begin with /l/. What meal begins with /l/?

Monitor Comprehension

1. **Is this story real or make-believe? How can you tell?** *(Possible response: This story is make-believe. The worm is carrying a picnic basket and has a picnic with the bug.)* **CRITICAL: DISTINGUISH BETWEEN FANTASY AND REALITY**

2. **What happens first, next, and last as a flower grows?** *(First a stem pops up. Next a leaf grows. Last the flower grows.)* **INFERENTIAL: SEQUENCE**

3. **Do you think *Spring Pops Up* is a good title for this book? Why or why not?** *(Children's responses should include reasons based on the text or the illustrations.)* **CRITICAL: MAKE JUDGMENTS**

Write in Response to Reading

Have children draw a picture of a flower. Help them name the parts of a flower (*stem, leaf,* and *flower*) that were used in the story. Write the terms on the board and have children use them to label their drawings.

All Fall Down
by Bill E. Neder

Summary

The circus clowns and animals build a pyramid that tumbles down when the last animal climbs on.

Introduce the Book

PICTURE WALK Have children turn through the pages of *All Fall Down*. Ask *Who climbed up next?* as each illustration is shared. Make sure children are familiar with all the animal names. Then ask children to predict what might happen when all the animals climb up. **PREDICT/SET PURPOSE**

Guided Reading

Page 2 **FOCUS STRATEGY** *Use Picture Clues to Confirm Meaning* Readers can often use the pictures to confirm words. Use the following prompts to support the reading of the word *tigers*.

You said *cats*. Look at the picture. Does that make sense? Does *cats* begin with *t*? What word begins with /t/t and makes sense?

Page 8 **FOCUS STRATEGY** *Look for Words You Know* Use the following prompts to coach the reading of the word *fall*.

Do you know a word that looks like this? You know *all*. What would it be if I added the letter *f* to the beginning?

Monitor Comprehension

1. **Tell what happened in this story.** (*The animals and clowns kept climbing on top of each other until they all fell down.*) **INFERENTIAL: SUMMARIZE**

2. **What clues on page 6 show that something bad is about to happen?** (*Possible responses: The wavy lines show that they are shaking. The animals and clowns look worried.*) **INFERENTIAL: MAKE PREDICTIONS**

3. **Why do you think the monkey is smiling on page 8?** (*Responses will vary.*) **CRITICAL: INTERPRET CHARACTERS' MOTIVATIONS**

Write in Response to Reading

Write the words *up* and *down* on the board. Ask what these words are called. (*opposites* or *antonyms*) Invite children to name other pairs of opposites, such as *in/out, hot/cold, happy/sad*. Have children choose and illustrate an antonym pair. Then have them label their pictures.

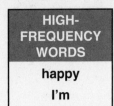
Just Like You!

by Jean Groce

Summary

A girl tries on hats and compares herself with various animals.

Introduce the Book

PICTURE WALK Hold up the book and read aloud the title, *Just Like You!*
Conduct a picture walk, helping children realize that the girl is looking into a
mirror. Ask them to identify and describe the animals. Have children read to
find out what the girl is doing. **PREDICT/SET PURPOSE**

Guided Reading

Page 3 **FOCUS STRATEGY** *Use Picture Clues to Confirm Meaning* Readers can often use
pictures to confirm words. Use the following prompts to coach the
reading of the word *tall*.

**You said ____. Look at the picture. Does that make sense? What is special
about a giraffe? What word would make sense?**

Page 6 **FOCUS STRATEGY** *Reread Aloud* Use the following prompts to coach the reading of
the word *shy*.

**Where's the tricky word? Look at the beginning. Look at the end. Think
about what would make sense. Reread the sentence and try that word.**

Monitor Comprehension

1. **What is the little girl doing in this story?** (*Possible response: She is
   trying on hats and looking in a mirror.*) **INFERENTIAL: GENERALIZE**

2. **Why are there animals in the mirror?** (*The girl is imagining she looks
   like these animals.*) **INFERENTIAL: DETERMINE THEME**

3. **Which hat is your favorite? Tell why.** (*Responses will vary.*) **CRITICAL:
   EXPRESS PERSONAL OPINIONS**

Write in Response to Reading

Have children write or dictate a sentence comparing themselves with an
animal by completing the sentence frame *I'm ____ like a ____.* Then have
children illustrate their sentences.

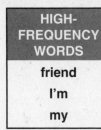

HIGH-
FREQUENCY
WORDS

friend

I'm

my

My Sister Is My Friend

by Hannah Markley

Summary

A little boy is glad that his sister is his friend, especially since she helps him find things.

Introduce the Book

PICTURE WALK Read the title of the book aloud. Ask children to tell ways they know that brothers and sisters can be friends. Then ask how brothers and sisters can help each other. As you turn through the book, discuss what is happening in the pictures. Have children read to find out why the boy is glad that his sister is his friend. **PREDICT/SET PURPOSE**

Guided Reading

Page 3   **FOCUS STRATEGY** *Use Picture Clues to Confirm Meaning* Readers know they can use pictures to confirm words as they read. Use the following prompts to coach the reading of the word *shoes*.

Check the picture. What do the boy and girl see under the bed?

Page 8   **FOCUS STRATEGY** *Self-Correct* When a word does not make sense, readers often realize they made a mistake and correct it on their own. Use the following prompts to support the reading of the word *glad*.

You said *I'm good*, and then you changed it to *I'm glad*. How did you know the word was *glad*?

Monitor Comprehension

1. **How is the girl helping her little brother?** *(She is helping him find things.)* **LITERAL: NOTE DETAILS**

2. **How do you think the girl feels about the snake? How can you tell?** *(Possible response: I think the girl does not like the snake because of the way she looks and the way she is holding it.)* **INFERENTIAL: DETERMINE CHARACTERS' EMOTIONS**

3. **Why do you think the girl is helping her brother?** *(Possible response: The girl loves her brother and likes to do things for him.)* **CRITICAL: INTERPRET CHARACTERS' MOTIVATIONS**

Write in Response to Reading

Have children discuss how sisters, brothers, or other family members are good friends. Help them write a letter in which they tell a family member why he or she is a good friend.

What Could It Be?

by Jennifer Jacobson

Summary

It's not a snake, a bird, or a bear in the bushes—it's a neighbor!

Introduce the Book

PICTURE WALK Read the title of the book and discuss the cover illustration. Point out the hedge with the leaves flying above it. As you have children look through the pictures, use questions such as *What do you think this could be?* Have children read to find out what the boy finds. **PREDICT/SET PURPOSE**

Guided Reading

Page 3 **FOCUS STRATEGY** *Use Picture Clues to Confirm Meaning* Readers know they can use pictures to confirm words as they read. Use the following prompts to coach the reading of the word *snake*.

Check the picture. What does the boy see? What animal might he think it looks like?

Page 4 **FOCUS STRATEGY** *Look for Words You Know* Readers can often determine a word by thinking about other, similar-looking words they know. Use the following prompts to support the reading of the word *not*.

This word ends with *ot*. What other words do you know that end with *ot*? How might that help you read this?

Monitor Comprehension

1. **Why do you think the boy is puzzled by what he sees?** *(He can only see part of each thing.)* **INFERENTIAL: DRAW CONCLUSIONS**

2. **How do you think the boy feels about what he sees? How can you tell?** *(Possible response: I think he is a little frightened because of the expression on his face and the way he sort of hunches down.)* **INFERENTIAL: DETERMINE CHARACTERS' EMOTIONS**

3. **How do you think the boy feels when he finds out what is behind the hedge?** *(Possible response: He is glad to know that it is only a friend behind the hedge and not something scary.)* **INFERENTIAL: DETERMINE CHARACTERS' EMOTIONS**

Write in Response to Reading

Have children draw an animal on a piece of paper. Have them cut a small hole in another sheet of paper and place it over the drawing so that part of the picture shows through the hole. Have them write the question *What can it be?* on the top sheet of paper. Provide time for children to share their work with classmates.

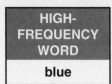
Butterflies

by Clara Reiff

Summary

This rhyming text explores the colors of butterflies.

Introduce the Book

PICTURE WALK Display the cover of the book and read the title. As children turn the pages, ask them to describe the butterflies they see, noting the colors. Have children read to discover many types of butterflies. **PREDICT/SET PURPOSE**

Guided Reading

Page 2 **FOCUS STRATEGY** *Use Picture Clues to Confirm Meaning* Readers know they can use pictures to confirm words as they read. Use the following prompts to coach the reading of the word *orange.*

Look at the word. Check the picture. What would you say this word is? Does that make sense? What color is it? That's right, this word names the color.

Page 5 **FOCUS STRATEGY** *Reread Aloud* Use the following prompts to support the reading of the word *two.*

What do you think the word is? Read the sentence again. Think about what would make sense. Try your word.

Monitor Comprehension

1. **Is this story about real butterflies or about make-believe ones? How can you tell?** *(These are real butterflies. They are photographs.)* **CRITICAL: DISTINGUISH BETWEEN FANTASY AND REALITY**

2. **In what ways are all the butterflies alike? How are they different?** *(The butterflies all have wings, legs, and feelers. They have different colors, shapes, and markings.)* **INFERENTIAL: COMPARE AND CONTRAST**

3. **Which butterfly is your favorite?** *(Responses will vary.)* **CRITICAL: EXPRESS PERSONAL OPINIONS**

Write in Response to Reading

Have children draw a butterfly in their favorite color. Then have them write the caption *Butterfly [color],* as in the book.

The Baby

by Gail Tuchman

Summary

The older brother watches the baby play with his things, and then joins in and plays with the baby.

Introduce the Book

PICTURE WALK Display the cover of the book and read the title. Ask children to look through the pictures and tell what is happening. Ask children to tell how they think the boy feels about the baby. **PREDICT/SET PURPOSE**

Guided Reading

Page 2 **FOCUS STRATEGY** *Read Ahead* Readers know they can read ahead to confirm a word. Use the following prompts to support the reading of the word *baby*.

You said ____. Then, when you read the rest of the sentence, you changed it to *baby*. I like the way you read ahead and discovered that the sentence is telling about the baby.

Page 3 **FOCUS STRATEGY** *Reread Aloud* Readers often reread to clarify meaning or to confirm a pattern. Use the following prompts to confirm the rhyme pattern.

Yes, the word is *lock*. Let's read both pages together. What can you tell me about the words *block* and *lock*? What can you predict about the next pages?

Monitor Comprehension

1. **Who is telling this story? How do you know?** (*The boy is telling the story. He says* the baby has my.) **INFERENTIAL: TEXT STRUCTURE**

2. **How do you think the boy feels about the baby taking his things? How can you tell?** (*Possible response: The boy does not like the baby taking his things. He looks sad and on page 5 he looks angry.*) **INFERENTIAL: DETERMINE CHARACTERS' EMOTIONS**

3. **How does the boy feel about the baby at the end of the story? What makes him change?** (*Possible response: The boy likes the baby because the baby is playing with him.*) **INFERENTIAL: DETERMINE CHARACTERS' EMOTIONS**

Write in Response to Reading

Invite children to tell about activities they enjoy with brothers, sisters, or other family members. Ask them to draw a picture that shows a fun family activity, and have them write a sentence about the picture.

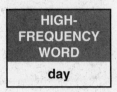
Bird's Bad Day

by Mercedes Ayers

Summary

Branches keep breaking, causing Bird to have a bad day.

Introduce the Book

PICTURE WALK Display the cover of the book and read the title. Ask children to speculate about what might cause a bird to have a bad day. As children look through the pictures, have them tell what is happening. Then ask children to read the story to find out what happens to Bird. **PREDICT/SET PURPOSE**

Guided Reading

Page 3   **FOCUS STRATEGY** *Self-Correct* Readers know when they have made a mistake and will often correct it on their own. Use the following prompts to support the reading.

You said ____ . Then you corrected your mistake. I like the way you used the meaning of the sentence to correct yourself.

Page 4   **FOCUS STRATEGY** *Use Picture Clues to Confirm Meaning* Readers know that the pictures can help to confirm words. Use the following prompts to confirm the word *nest*.

How did you know that the word was *nest*? It's good that you knew that the words should match the picture.

Monitor Comprehension

1. **Why did Bird have a bad day?** *(Every time Bird was on a branch, it broke.)* **INFERENTIAL: GENERALIZE**

2. **How would you feel if you were Bird?** *(Possible responses: angry or sad)* **CRITICAL: IDENTIFY WITH CHARACTERS**

3. **What do you think would happen if Bird landed on a tree branch to sing?** *(Possible response: The branch would break.)* **INFERENTIAL: SPECULATE**

Write in Response to Reading

Discuss with children what they think might happen to Bird on a good day. Ask them to think of things Bird might say in each situation. Then have them illustrate and write about something that might happen to Bird on a good day.

The Perfect Pet
by Cheyenne Cisco

Summary

The perfect pet for this family is one that won't make anyone sneeze.

Introduce the Book

PICTURE WALK Read the title and show the cover to children. Discuss where the family is and what kinds of pets they see. Then, as children look through the pictures, discuss what problems they think the family has in picking a pet. Ask children to read to find out whether or not the family finds a pet. **PREDICT/SET PURPOSE**

Guided Reading

Page 2 **FOCUS STRATEGY** *Reread Aloud* Readers often read a passage again to give it greater expression. Use the following prompts to support rereading the first page.

Good, you read all the words. Now, how do you think this would sound if the boy were speaking? Look at the picture. Is this a quiet little sneeze? Read it again and try to make it sound as if the boy is speaking.

Page 5 **FOCUS STRATEGY** *Use Picture Clues to Confirm Meaning* Readers know that the pictures can help to confirm words. Use the following prompts to confirm the word *mouse*.

How did you know that the word was *mouse*? What word clue told you this was *mouse* instead of *mice*?

Monitor Comprehension

1. **What problem did the family have?** *(All the pets made someone in the family sneeze.)* **INFERENTIAL: CAUSE-EFFECT**

2. **How do you think the boys and their dad feel about their pet?** *(Possible response: They are happy to find a pet that does not make anyone sneeze.)* **INFERENTIAL: DRAW CONCLUSIONS**

3. **What do you think the boys' mother will say when she sees this pet?** *(Responses will vary.)* **CRITICAL: SPECULATE**

Write in Response to Reading

Have children look again at the pet on page 8. Discuss what kind of animal they think this might be. Encourage them to tell how the boys should take care of it. Then have children draw a house for this pet and give the pet a name. Ask them to write a sentence telling something the boys might do with this pet.

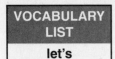
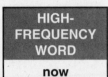
"Help!" Said Jed

by Deborah Eaton

Summary

This is a "noodle head" tale. It deals with kindly characters who lack good sense. When Jed gets stuck in a tree, it takes his whole family to get him down.

Introduce the Book

PICTURE WALK Display the cover and read the title. Ask why children think Jed needs help. Have children turn several pages and tell about what is happening in the pictures. Ask children to read to find out what happens when people try to help Jed. **PREDICT/SET PURPOSE**

Guided Reading

Page 5 **FOCUS STRATEGY** *Self-Correct* When a reader can tell that a word has been read incorrectly, he or she will often correct the word by studying it more closely.

You said ____ . Then you looked at the word more closely and changed it to ____ . I like the way you used the letters of the word to figure out the word.

Page 7 **FOCUS STRATEGY** *Use Picture Clues to Confirm Meaning* Readers know that the pictures can help to confirm words. Use the following prompts to confirm the word *Thanks*.

What clues in the picture helped you know the word was *Thanks*? Did you think about what someone should say when they are helped?

Monitor Comprehension

1. **How did Jed's family try to help him?** *(They climbed on top of one another until they could finally reach Jed.)* **INFERENTIAL: SUMMARIZE**

2. **What problem did Jed's family have at the end of the story?** *(They were stuck in the tree and didn't know how to get down.)* **INFERENTIAL: SEQUENCE**

3. **What do you think happened next to Jed's family?** *(Responses will vary.)* **CRITICAL: SPECULATE**

Write in Response to Reading

Have children think about what might happen if Jed needed help to carry a big box. Have them draw a picture and write a sentence about how the family helps Jed with the box.

HIGH-
FREQUENCY
WORDS

here

little

mother

one

this

One More Time

by Ben Farrell

Summary

Children at an amusement park try to find a ride they will all enjoy.

Introduce the Book

PICTURE WALK   Share the title and cover illustration. Help children identify the roll of tickets and ask where this story takes place. As children look at the pictures, have them describe what is happening. Ask them to read to find out what the children might do "one more time." **PREDICT/SET PURPOSE**

Guided Reading

Page 4   **FOCUS STRATEGY**   *Use Picture Clues to Confirm Meaning* Readers know that the text should match the pictures. Use the following prompts to confirm the reading of page 4.

I like the way you noticed who is talking in this picture. How did that help you read the page?

Page 6   **FOCUS STRATEGY**   *Self-Correct* Readers often correct their own mistakes when reading. Use the following prompts to support this.

You said ____ , and then you changed it. How did you know the word was ____ ?

Monitor Comprehension

1. **Why are the children having trouble choosing a ride?** *(Their mother said they could only ride one, and they are all different sizes.)* **INFERENTIAL: SUMMARIZE**

2. **What ride did they finally choose? How do you know?** *(They chose a merry-go-round. The horses are from a merry-go-round.)* **CRITICAL: AUTHOR'S CRAFT/INTERPRET IMAGERY**

3. **Why do you think this story is called *One More Time*?** *(After the characters choose a ride, they get to ride it one more time.)* **CRITICAL: AUTHOR'S CRAFT**

Write in Response to Reading

Have children choose a favorite ride from the story or another one they like. Ask them to create a poster for their ride by drawing a picture of it and labeling it with the following sentence:

This ____ ride is the one for me.

Children can complete the sentence with an appropriate adjective, such as *big, fast, exciting, little, slow,* etc.

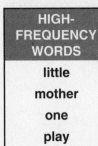
Where Babies Play

by Hayley Novak

Summary

Each kind of baby has its own place to play.

Introduce the Book

PICTURE WALK Share the cover and title with children. Ask what kind of baby they see on the cover. Ask where children think this baby plays. As children look at the pictures, have them tell what baby is playing. Then ask children to read to find out where each little one plays. **PREDICT/SET PURPOSE**

Guided Reading

Page 2 **FOCUS STRATEGY** *Look for Word Bits and Parts* Readers can often find a familiar or easily decodable part of a word that will help them read the word. Use the following prompts to support reading the word *little*.

Look at just the first three letters. How should this part of the word sound? Now look at the end of the word and put the two parts together.

Page 3 **FOCUS STRATEGY** *Use Picture Clues to Confirm Meaning* Readers know that the text should match the pictures. Use the following prompts to support the reading of page 3.

What do we call the place where pigs live? How does knowing that help you read this page?

Monitor Comprehension

1. **What animal baby did you see first? Next? After that?** *(First was a pig, next was a duck, and after that was a bear.)* **LITERAL: SEQUENCE**

2. **Which baby would you like to play with? Why?** *(Responses will vary.)* **CRITICAL: EXPRESS PERSONAL OPINIONS**

3. **Can you name another baby animal? Follow the question-and-answer format from the book to tell where your animal plays.** *(Responses will vary.)* **CRITICAL: EXTEND STORY**

Write in Response to Reading

Discuss with children other baby animals they know, such as chick, calf, duckling, piglet, pup, kitten. Then tell children they can help make a book about baby animals that is similar to *Where Babies Play*. Choose an activity, such as sleep. Have children choose a baby animal, and then draw and write about it for the book. You may want to write the sentence pattern on the board for them, for example: *Where does this little one sleep? on a pillow*

VOCABULARY LIST

mix

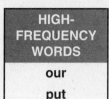

HIGH-FREQUENCY WORDS

our

put

Friendship Salad

by Lynn Trepicchio

Summary

Each friend brings a favorite fruit to combine into friendship salad.

Introduce the Book

PICTURE WALK Share the cover and title with children. As children turn the pages, have them name the kinds of fruit they see. Then ask them to predict what a friendship salad might be. **PREDICT/SET PURPOSE**

Guided Reading

Page 2 **FOCUS STRATEGY** *Use Picture Clues to Confirm Meaning* Readers know they can use the pictures to help them identify words. Use the following prompt to reinforce the reading of the word *bananas.*

Good, you knew from looking at the picture what word made sense in the sentence.

Page 6 **FOCUS STRATEGY** *Self-Correct* When a mistake that does not make sense is made, good readers will go back and restate the sentence, correcting the missed word.

You said ____ . Then you changed it to ____ . When the sentence did not make sense, you fixed the word that gave you trouble. That's a good thing to do when you read.

Monitor Comprehension

1. **What kind of salad is the friendship salad?** *(It's a fruit salad.)* **LITERAL: NOTE DETAILS**

2. **Why do you think this salad is called a friendship salad?** *(Possible response: Each friend brought something to help make the salad.)* **CRITICAL: INTERPRET STORY EVENTS**

3. **Which fruits are from warm places? How can you tell?** *(Possible response: Bananas and pineapples come from warm places. I can tell by the clothing of the children bringing these fruits as well as the palm trees in the illustrations.)* **CRITICAL: CLASSIFY**

Write in Response to Reading

Discuss with children ingredients they might like to put in their own friendship salad. Then have them write or dictate the steps to make the salad. Have each child choose an ingredient and draw it. Use their pictures to illustrate the recipe.

Garden Birthday

by Deborah Kaye

Summary

Everyone in the garden has a special kind of birthday cake.

Introduce the Book

PICTURE WALK Display the book cover and read the title. Discuss what children might expect to see at a garden birthday party. As children look through the pictures, have them name the animals and predict what kind of cake each animal might like. **PREDICT/SET PURPOSE**

Guided Reading

Page 2 **FOCUS STRATEGY** *Use Picture Clues to Confirm Meaning* Readers use pictures to help them identify words. Use the following prompts to reinforce the reading of the page.

What do you know about squirrels that helped you read this page? What clues did you find in the picture for each word?

Page 4 **FOCUS STRATEGY** *Self-Correct* Readers who rely heavily on picture clues may look at a word and realize it does not match what they said. Use the following prompts to support this strategy.

You said ____ . Then you changed it to ____ . How did you know?

Monitor Comprehension

1. **What clues can you find in the pictures that tell you each picture is a birthday party?** *(Possible response: The characters are wearing party hats and have a cake.)* **INFERENTIAL: IMPORTANT DETAILS**

2. **Is this story real or make-believe? How can you tell?** *(The story is make-believe. Animals don't wear party hats and eat cakes.)* **CRITICAL: DISTINGUISH BETWEEN FANTASY AND REALITY**

3. **Which cake would you most like to taste? Why?** *(Responses will vary.)* **CRITICAL: EXPRESS PERSONAL OPINIONS**

Write in Response to Reading

Discuss animals children know and ingredients that might be put in a cake for each animal. Have them select an animal and draw it with its cake. Then have them write a sentence about the picture.

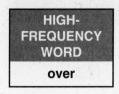

Good-bye, Fox

by Catherine James

Summary

While chasing a fox, the dog has to jump over many things, including a cat.

Introduce the Book

PICTURE WALK Display the book cover and read the title. Discuss who children think is saying good-bye to the fox. Have children turn through the pages and tell what is happening in the pictures. Then have them read to find out how the dog chases the fox. **PREDICT/SET PURPOSE**

Guided Reading

Page 2   **FOCUS STRATEGY**   *Reread Aloud* Once readers are sure of the words, rereading a section aloud encourages them to read expressively.

What do you know about the mark at the end of this sentence? If you were the dog, how would you say this? Show me how the dog would sound.

Page 4   **FOCUS STRATEGY**   *Use Picture Clues to Confirm Meaning* Readers can use the pictures to support word identification. Use these prompts to reinforce children's use of the pictures.

What is the dog jumping over? Do you see the word *gate* in the text? I like the way you looked at the picture to make sure the words matched.

Monitor Comprehension

1. **Why do you think the dog is chasing the fox?** *(Possible response: Dogs like to chase other animals.)* **CRITICAL: INTERPRET CHARACTERS' MOTIVATIONS**

2. **How do you think the cat feels about the dog jumping over it?** *(Possible response: The cat is surprised, judging from the expression on its face.)* **INFERENTIAL: DETERMINE CHARACTERS' EMOTIONS**

3. **Why did the dog say "good-bye" to the fox?** *(Responses will vary.)* **CRITICAL: INTERPRET CHARACTERS' MOTIVATIONS**

Write in Response to Reading

Have children pretend that the fox came to a different place, such as the seashore, a play yard, or a school. Ask them to name things the dog may jump over in this location. Have children complete the sentence *Jump over the* ____. Then have them illustrate their sentence.

After Goldilocks

by Johanna Richard

Summary

This is an extension of the traditional story. After the visit from
Goldilocks, all Baby Bear has left are kisses from his parents.

Introduce the Book

PICTURE WALK Discuss with children the story *The Three Bears*. Tell or read
it if children are unfamiliar with the story events. Then have them read to find
out what might happen after Goldilocks has left the Bears' house.
PREDICT/SET PURPOSE

Guided Reading

Page 3 **FOCUS STRATEGY** *Self-Correct* Readers recognize when a misread word does not
make sense and will correct the word on their own. Use the
following prompts to reinforce this strategy.

**You said ____. Then you changed it to ____. How did you know to change
it? How did you know when you had the right word?**

Page 6 **FOCUS STRATEGY** *Look for Word Bits and Parts* Readers can find parts of words that
they can read. These parts can help them determine the longer
word. Use these prompts to support the reading of the word *kisses*.

**Look at all the letters. Do you see any part of this word that you already
know? Does that give you a hint about this word?**

Monitor Comprehension

1. **How do you think Baby Bear feels about his bowl and his chair? How
   can you tell?** *(Possible response: Baby Bear feels sad. I can tell because
   of the expression on his face.)* **INFERENTIAL: DETERMINE CHARACTERS'
   EMOTIONS**

2. **How have Baby Bear's feelings changed on pages 4 and 5? What
   caused them to change?** *(Possible response: Baby Bear is happy now
   because he is playing.)* **INFERENTIAL: CAUSE-EFFECT**

3. **What happened when Baby Bear started jumping on the bed?** *(Mother
   and Father Bear got up, tucked him in, and kissed him good night. Then
   they all went to sleep.)* **INFERENTIAL: RETELL**

Write in Response to Reading

Discuss with children what kinds of signs the bear family might like to post
outside its home after Goldilocks has left. Have children create signs with
messages that could be posted by the bears.

One Little Slip

by Gail Tuchman

Summary

Little Hippo's slip causes the whole family to get wet.

Introduce the Book

PICTURE WALK Share the cover and title of the book with children. Have them preview the illustrations on pages 2–7 and tell what is happening. Then ask children to read to find out what happens when Little Hippo makes one little slip. **PREDICT/SET PURPOSE**

Guided Reading

Page 3   **FOCUS STRATEGY**   *Look for Words You Know* Readers can use words that they know to help them read words with similar spellings. Use the following prompts to support the reading of rhyming words.

The last word in the first sentence was *trip*. Now change the beginning to *sl*. Say the two rhyming words.

Page 4   **FOCUS STRATEGY**   *Self-Correct* Readers often can determine when a misread word does not make sense and will correct the word on their own. The following prompts will reinforce this strategy.

You said ____. Then you changed it to ____. How did you know the first word was wrong? How did you know when you had the right word?

Monitor Comprehension

1. **Tell what happened to the Hippo family.** (*Little Hippo slipped, then Mother Hippo flipped, then Father Hippo tipped and they all ended up in the water.*) **INFERENTIAL: RETELL**

2. **Do you think *One Little Slip* is a good name for this story? Why?** (*Possible response: Yes. The one little slip by Little Hippo causes everyone to fall into the water.*) **CRITICAL: MAKE JUDGMENTS**

3. **How do you think the hippos feel about being in the water? How can you tell?** (*Possible response: They seem to be happy in the water because they are all smiling.*) **INFERENTIAL: DETERMINE CHARACTERS' EMOTIONS**

Write in Response to Reading

Invite children to suggest silly things that might happen to other animal families. Have them draw pictures showing a family doing something silly and then write some sentences that tell about the picture.

My Family Band

by Ben Farrell

Summary

When every member of the family plays an instrument, they can join together and have a band.

Introduce the Book

PICTURE WALK Share the cover and title of the book with children. Point out the word *band,* and explain that this word can have more than one meaning. Discuss the meanings children know, and ask what kind of band they think they will find in this book. Then have children turn through the book, and help them identify the various instruments. Ask them to read to find out what happens when this family gets together. **PREDICT/SET PURPOSE**

Guided Reading

Pages 2–3 **FOCUS STRATEGY** *Use Picture Clues to Confirm Meaning* Readers know that the words they read should match what they see in the pictures. Use the following prompts to support children using the pictures to identify words.

Look at the picture. Who do you think this family member is? What instrument do you see?

Page 6 **FOCUS STRATEGY** *Reread Aloud* Rereading increases fluency and understanding. Prompt children to return to previous pages and to read them again.

Let's see what we've learned so far. Turn back and reread the pages.

Monitor Comprehension

1. **Who are the band members and what do they play?** *(Grandpa plays piano, Grandma plays violin, Father plays guitar, Mother plays tuba, Uncle plays a horn, and the boy plays the drum.)* **INFERENTIAL: SUMMARIZE**

2. **Who is telling the story? How can you tell?** *(The boy playing the drum is telling the story because he uses* I *when he tells about himself.)* **CRITICAL: INTERPRET TEXT STRUCTURE**

3. **Would you like to be a member of this family? Why or why not?** *(Responses will vary.)* **CRITICAL: EXPRESS PERSONAL OPINIONS**

Write in Response to Reading

Have children think about instruments they might like to play. Then have them draw themselves playing an instrument and complete the sentence ____ *will be there with a* ____. Collect the pages into a book called *Our Class Band.*

VOCABULARY LIST

mouse

wanted

HIGH-FREQUENCY WORDS

much

so

very

What Is in the Box?

by Lucy McClymont

Summary

A boy learns that the surprise in the box is just what he wanted.

Introduce the Book

PICTURE WALK Show the book and read the title. As children preview the pictures, ask them to tell what they see in the box. Ask them to read to find out what the boy finds in the box. **PREDICT/SET PURPOSE**

Guided Reading

Page 3   **FOCUS STRATEGY** *Use Picture Clues to Confirm Meaning* Readers know that the words in the text match what they see in the pictures. Use the following prompts to support children using the pictures to identify words.

Look at the picture. What do you see sticking out of the box? What will the boy say if this is all he can see?

Page 6   **FOCUS STRATEGY** *Reread Aloud* Reading with expression can increase fluency and enjoyment by making the text sound like spoken words. Use the following prompts to encourage children to read aloud with expression.

Look at the boy's face. Does he look excited? Read the words aloud and try to make them sound as if the boy is speaking.

Monitor Comprehension

1. **What did the boy see that helped him guess what was in the box?** *(First he saw ears, then eyes, then a nose, then a tail.)* **INFERENTIAL: SUMMARIZE**

2. **Was a mouse a good guess? Why or why not?** *(Responses will vary.)* **CRITICAL: MAKE JUDGMENTS**

3. **How does the boy feel about his present? How can you tell?** *(Possible response: He's very happy. He is smiling and he says, "I wanted one so much.")* **INFERENTIAL: DETERMINE CHARACTERS' EMOTIONS**

Write in Response to Reading

Have children fold a piece of paper in half to make a booklet. Have them draw an object on the inside, and on the front write two or three hints about the object. Below the hints they can write *What is it?* Have them work with a partner to read the hints and try to guess what the partner has drawn.

VOCABULARY LIST

gave
wanted

HIGH-FREQUENCY WORDS

much
so
very

Four Very Big Beans

by Lucy Floyd

Summary

In this counting book a girl gives away three of the four very big beans on her plate.

Introduce the Book

PICTURE WALK Display the cover, read the title, and have children find the four beans in the picture. Have children look through the pictures and tell what is happening. Then ask them to read to find out what problem the little girl has. **PREDICT/SET PURPOSE**

Guided Reading

Page 2 **FOCUS STRATEGY** *Use Picture Clues to Confirm Meaning* Readers know that the words should tell about the pictures. Use the following prompts to support children who need the pictures to identify words.

Look at the picture. What is on the girl's plate? How many do you see? Now let's read the words.

Page 5 **FOCUS STRATEGY** *Reread Aloud* Reading with expression can increase enjoyment and improve fluency. Use the following prompts to encourage children to read with expression.

What mark do you see at the end of the sentences on the first line? What does this mark mean? How do you think the girl sounds if she is excited? Read the words aloud and try to make them sound like the girl is speaking.

Monitor Comprehension

1. **What was the girl's problem in this story?** *(She did not want to eat all her beans.)* **INFERENTIAL: SUMMARIZE**

2. **Why did the girl wrap a bean as a present for her grandma?** *(Possible response: She wanted her grandma to think the bean was a present and take it.)* **INFERENTIAL: DRAW CONCLUSIONS**

3. **Who did the girl give beans to first, next, and last?** *(first to Grandma, next to Sue, and last to her mom)* **INFERENTIAL: SEQUENCE**

Write in Response to Reading

Have children draw a picture of a favorite food and write a caption for their drawing. Suggest that children use number words to describe the drawing, such as two slices of pizza, three scoops of ice cream, or five cookies.

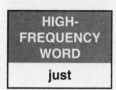
I Was Just About to Go to Bed

by Lucy McClymont

Summary

When a girl finally gathers all the things she needs to take to bed, there is no longer any room for her.

Introduce the Book

PICTURE WALK Display the cover of the book and read the title. Ask what special preparations children make before they go to bed. Have them turn through the pictures and tell what they see. Then suggest they read to find out how the girl gets ready for bed. **PREDICT/SET PURPOSE**

Guided Reading

Page 3   **FOCUS STRATEGY** *Look for Word Bits and Parts* Readers can look for parts that they can read in longer words and use the parts to help identify the whole word. Use these prompts to help children look for word parts they can read.

That's a long word. Look at just the first few letters. Can you read this part? Now look at the rest of the word. Put both parts together and read the word. Does your word make sense?

Page 5   **FOCUS STRATEGY** *Self-Correct* When a word is misread and the misread word does not make sense, readers will often correct the mistake on their own. Use the following prompts to support the correction of errors.

At first you said ____. Then you changed it to ____. Why did you change it? What clues told you that the first word was not right?

Monitor Comprehension

1. **Do you think this girl was very sleepy? Why or why not?** *(Possible response: No. She kept finding reasons not to go to bed.)* **INFERENTIAL: DRAW CONCLUSIONS**

2. **What is the girl's problem at the end of the story? How do you think she might solve it?** *(She has too many things in her bed. Responses will vary.)* **CRITICAL: SPECULATE**

3. **How are you like this girl at bedtime? How are you different?** *(Responses will vary.)* **CRITICAL: IDENTIFY WITH CHARACTERS**

Write in Response to Reading

Discuss with children activities they do regularly, such as get ready for school, go to soccer practice, or go to a baby-sitter. Have them think of what they need to get ready and write a list. Then have them illustrate each item on the list.

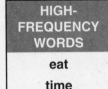

What Time Is It?

by Jeanette Mara

Summary

Ann has a new watch that she proudly shows off to her special friends.

Introduce the Book

PICTURE WALK Display the cover of the book and read the title. Have children look at the cover picture and predict why the book has this title. As children preview the pictures, discuss who the girl's friends are and what they are doing. Suggest that children read to find out how Ann uses her new watch. **PREDICT/SET PURPOSE**

Guided Reading

Pages 2–3 **FOCUS STRATEGY** *Use Picture Clues to Confirm Meaning* Readers can use the pictures to verify words they read. Use the following prompts to affirm children's use of picture clues.

You said ____. Look at the picture. Does your word make sense?

Page 8 **FOCUS STRATEGY** *Self-Correct* Readers often choose words that make sense but that are not correct. Use the following prompts to support the correction of errors.

At first you said ____. Then you changed it to ____. Why did you change it? What clues told you that you were not right the first time?

Monitor Comprehension

1. **How do you think Ann feels about her watch? How can you tell?** *(Possible response: She is very proud of her watch. She shows it to all her friends and uses it all the time.)* **INFERENTIAL: DETERMINE CHARACTERS' EMOTIONS**

2. **How can you tell that Ann is a very helpful person?** *(She helps the animals by feeding them. She helps her parents by feeding the baby and helping to get dinner ready.)* **METACOGNITIVE: DETERMINE CHARACTERS' TRAITS**

3. **How would having a watch be helpful to you?** *(Responses will vary.)* **CRITICAL: EXPRESS PERSONAL OPINIONS**

Write in Response to Reading

Discuss with children favorite activities and the times they occur. Have children choose an activity and illustrate it. Then have them write the question *What time is it?* and complete the sentence frame *It's time to ____.*

VOCABULARY LIST
fork

HIGH-FREQUENCY WORDS
know
table

Know Your Birthday Manners

by Clara Reiff

Summary

A silly monkey learns good manners at his birthday party.

Introduce the Book

PICTURE WALK Display the book and read the title. As children preview the pictures, discuss what the monkey is doing. Point out that when the mother speaks, her words appear in a speech balloon. Suggest that children read to find out what the monkey learns. **PREDICT/SET PURPOSE**

Guided Reading

Page 3 **FOCUS STRATEGY** *Use Word Order and Context to Confirm Meaning* Readers can use the context of a sentence to verify a word. Use the following prompts to support children's use of context clues.

What do you think the monkey's mother wants to say to him? This is a book about good manners. What word should she use to be polite?

Page 5 **FOCUS STRATEGY** *Reread Aloud* Rereading aloud adds to the enjoyment of the text as it increases fluency. Use the following prompts to encourage the rereading of the mother's words.

How does the mother feel? How do you think she sounds when she talks to her little monkey? Can you reread this and make it sound the way she might sound?

Monitor Comprehension

1. **Why do you think the author put the words *do not* in dark capital letters?** *(Possible response: to make the words look very important)* **INFERENTIAL: AUTHOR'S CRAFT**

2. **What rules do you think the monkey should know about unwrapping presents?** *(Responses will vary.)* **CRITICAL: SPECULATE**

3. **Would you want this monkey to come to your birthday party? Why or why not?** *(Responses will vary.)* **CRITICAL: EXPRESS PERSONAL OPINIONS**

Write in Response to Reading

Invite children to brainstorm situations in which it is important to use good manners. Then title a sheet of chart paper *Know Your ____ Manners*. Invite children to add rules to the chart. Suggest that they begin rules with *Do* or *Please*.

HIGH-
FREQUENCY
WORDS

room

table

All I Did

by Lucy Floyd

Summary

A boy finds many ways to entertain himself, but each one seems to earn him a time out.

Introduce the Book

PICTURE WALK Display the book and read the title. Ask children to look at the cover picture and predict what this story might be about. Then, as children preview the pictures, discuss what the boy is doing. Then have children read to find out what happens to the boy. **PREDICT/SET PURPOSE**

Guided Reading

Page 3　**FOCUS STRATEGY** *Self-Correct* Readers who rely on picture clues may have trouble because the words *fix up my room* do not match what is happening in the picture. If children misread these words, the following prompts will help you support correcting of the error.

You are paying attention to the pictures, but look carefully at the words. What letter do you see at the beginning of the word after *was*?

Page 7　**FOCUS STRATEGY** *Reread Aloud* Rereading aloud invites the reader to interpret a character's words and express them in a way the character might. Use the following prompts to encourage rereading.

How does the boy feel? How do you think he sounds when he talks to his mother? What hint does the author give you?

Monitor Comprehension

1. **Look at page 3. What does the boy think he is doing? What does his mother think he is doing?** *(The boy thinks he is fixing up his room. His mother thinks he is making a mess.)* **INFERENTIAL: COMPARE/CONTRAST**

2. **Why does the boy's mom keep saying, "time out"?** *(Possible response: He keeps making messes.)* **INFERENTIAL: CAUSE-EFFECT**

3. **How do you know that Mom is not angry with the boy?** *(She hugs him.)* **CRITICAL: INTERPRET CHARACTERS' MOTIVATIONS**

Write in Response to Reading

Discuss with children things they may have done that made a mess. Have them illustrate their mess and complete the sentence frame *All I did was ____.*

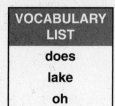
Frog's Day

by Catherine James

Summary

A frog has an extraordinary day as he listens to music, snacks, and sings in a band.

Introduce the Book

PICTURE WALK Share the title and cover of the book with children. Have them predict whether this book is about a real frog or an imaginary one. Confirm their predictions by having them preview the pictures and discuss what they see the frog doing. Then have children read to find out how Frog spends his day. **PREDICT/SET PURPOSE**

Guided Reading

Page 4 **FOCUS STRATEGY** *Use Picture Clues to Confirm Meaning* Readers can use the picture to confirm unfamiliar words. Use the following prompts to encourage the reading of the phrase *listen to music.*

Look at the frog. What is he wearing? What is he doing? What hint in the picture tells you that he is hearing music? Now read the sentence.

Page 7 **FOCUS STRATEGY** *Make Predictions* Use the following prompts to encourage children to predict what the frog will do next.

Can you find Frog in the picture? What are the other animals doing? What do you think Frog will do? What do you think Frog will say?

Monitor Comprehension

1. **What things does Frog do on this day?** *(He sleeps, takes a bath, eats a snack, listens to music, plays at the lake, and sings.)* **INFERENTIAL: SUMMARIZE**

2. **What does Frog do that a real frog does? What does he do that a real frog cannot do?** *(A real frog might rest and eat bugs. A real frog can't take a bath, listen to music, play an instrument, wear clothes, or sing with a microphone.)* **CRITICAL: DISTINGUISH BETWEEN FANTASY AND REALITY**

3. **What might Frog do next?** *(Responses will vary.)* **CRITICAL: SPECULATE**

Write in Response to Reading

Invite children to follow the story pattern to write about "Frog's Night." Have them brainstorm what Frog might do. Have each child draw and write about one thing Frog does at night.

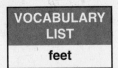

VOCABULARY LIST

feet

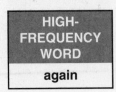

HIGH-FREQUENCY WORD

again

Famous Feet

by Hannah Markley

Summary

Take a look at the feet of some favorite storybook friends.

Introduce the Book

PICTURE WALK Share the title and cover of the book. Discuss what makes something or someone famous. Then ask for several suggestions of whose feet might be famous. Ask children to preview the pictures and tell whose feet they see in each picture. Then have children read to find out what kind of feet are famous. **PREDICT/SET PURPOSE**

Guided Reading

Page 3 **FOCUS STRATEGY** *Use Picture Clues to Confirm Meaning* The pictures can help children understand what they read. Use the following prompts to encourage the reading of the page.

Where are these feet? Who do you think this is? What is he doing?

Page 6 **FOCUS STRATEGY** *Self-Correct* When a word is misread, a reader will often catch the mistake and change the word. Use the following prompts to reinforce self-correction.

You first said _____, and then you changed it to _____. What made you change it? How did you know which word was right?

Monitor Comprehension

1. **Whose famous feet did you see in the book?** (*Cinderella's, Jack and the Beanstalk's, the Big Bad Wolf's, Baby Bear's, the Cow That Jumped Over the Moon's, and the Gingerbread Man's*) **CRITICAL: RECOGNIZE AUTHOR'S PURPOSE**

2. **Can you name another character that might fit one of the clues?** (*Possible responses: Sleeping Beauty/princess feet, giant/big bad feet, tortoise and hare/running feet*) **CRITICAL: CLASSIFY**

3. **Can you give another clue that might fit one of the characters?** (*Possible responses: Famous dancing feet/Cinderella, Famous jumping feet/cow, Famous baby feet/Baby Bear*) **CRITICAL: CLASSIFY**

Write in Response to Reading

Ask children to think about other story characters they know and the kinds of things the characters do. Have children write a sentence about one character and draw shoes the character might wear.

VOCABULARY
LIST

dancing
leaping
moving
turning

Dancing

by Lynn Trepicchio

Summary

Dancers perform many different actions.

Introduce the Book

PICTURE WALK Share the title and cover of the book. Ask children to preview the pictures and tell what the characters are doing. Discuss the actions of the dancers, introducing the words *leaping, turning,* and *listening*. Then have children read to find out what dancers do. **PREDICT/SET PURPOSE**

Guided Reading

Page 4   **FOCUS STRATEGY** *Self-Correct* Use the following prompts to guide a child who misreads *leaping*.

You said ____. I like the way you used the picture to help you read the words. The word begins with *l*. Does the word you said begin with *l*? Can you think of a word that begins with *l* and makes sense?

Page 8   **FOCUS STRATEGY** *Look for Word Bits and Parts* Readers can often find parts they know in words. Use the following prompts to guide the reading of *something*.

Look at the word. Can you find a part you know in this word? Can you find two words you know? Say the words together. What is this word?

Monitor Comprehension

1. **Are the dancers in this book real or make-believe? How can you tell?** *(They are real. The pictures are photographs.)* **CRITICAL: DISTINGUISH BETWEEN FANTASY AND REALITY**

2. **How are the dancers on pages 2 and 6 alike? How are they different?** *(Responses will vary.)* **INFERENTIAL: COMPARE AND CONTRAST**

3. **Which dance would you like to see? Why?** *(Responses will vary.)* **CRITICAL: EXPRESS PERSONAL OPINIONS**

Write in Response to Reading

Ask children to think about other activities in which people perform different actions, such as ice skating, swimming, or playing soccer. Have children write a sentence using the pattern from *Dancing* and illustrate it.

A Place for Nicholas

by Lucy Floyd

Summary

When Nicholas wants a place of his own, his little brother Jeff makes a perfect spot.

Introduce the Book

PICTURE WALK Share the title and cover of the book. Tell children that Nicholas has a problem; then ask which character on the cover they think is Nicholas. Have children look through pages 2–7 and tell about the pictures. Then have children read to find out how Nicholas's problem is solved. **PREDICT/SET PURPOSE**

Guided Reading

Page 3 **FOCUS STRATEGY** *Reread Aloud* Rereading a passage aloud may help a reader hear where he or she has misread a word. Use the following prompts to encourage children to reread aloud.

Read that sentence again. Which word was hard for you? Did your word make sense? Think about what would make sense. Now try your word in the sentence.

Page 5 **FOCUS STRATEGY** *Use Picture Clues to Confirm Meaning* Readers can use the pictures to confirm the meaning of a passage. Use these prompts to confirm the reading of the page.

Look at the picture. You said ——. Does that make sense? What would make more sense and tell about the picture?

Monitor Comprehension

1. **What problem did Nicholas have?** (*He wanted a special place all to himself.*) **LITERAL: NOTE DETAILS**

2. **What was wrong with each place his family suggested?** (*Someone else was there.*) **INFERENTIAL: GENERALIZE**

3. **How was Nicholas's problem solved?** (*His little brother Jeff and his mom used a blanket to separate Nicholas's bed from the rest of the room.*) **INFERENTIAL: SUMMARIZE**

Write in Response to Reading

Reread page 8 with children and have them brainstorm what Nicholas, Mom, or Jeff might say next. Have them write a sentence that one of the characters might say. Help them place the quotation marks correctly.

Old MacDonald's Fun Time Farm

by Gail Tuchman

Summary

Lively illustrations and text challenge children to locate unique farm animals.

Introduce the Book

PICTURE WALK Share the title and cover illustration with children. As they preview the illustrations, ask what is unusual about this farm. Explain that they will find a certain animal in each illustration. Then have them read the book to find the animals. **PREDICT/SET PURPOSE**

Guided Reading

Page 2 **FOCUS STRATEGY** *Use Picture Clues to Confirm Meaning* Readers can use the small pictures to confirm the last word in each sentence. Use these prompts to point out the small picture and to confirm the reading.

Look at the little animal after the sentence. What is it? Now read the question.

Page 8 **FOCUS STRATEGY** *Self-Correct* When working with patterned text, readers will notice when the pattern changes. They will often correct their reading on their own. The following prompts will help you reinforce this behavior.

When you started to read you said _____. Then you changed it to _____. What did you notice that helped you change your mind?

Monitor Comprehension

1. **Are these animals real or make-believe? How can you tell?** *(They are make-believe. They are doing things people do.)* **CRITICAL: DISTINGUISH BETWEEN FANTASY AND REALITY**

2. **Which activity would you like to do with the animals? Why?** *(Responses will vary.)* **CRITICAL: EXPRESS PERSONAL OPINIONS**

3. **Which animal was the hardest for you to find? Why?** *(Responses will vary.)* **METACOGNITIVE: MAKE COMPARISONS**

Write in Response to Reading

Have each child choose an object in the room, draw a picture of it, and complete the sentence frame *Can you find this ____ ?* Have children work with partners or in small groups to exchange papers, read the sentences, and find the objects.

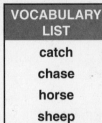

**VOCABULARY
LIST**

catch

chase

horse

sheep

Play Ball!

by Glen Harlan

Summary

The neighborhood critters have a fine time playing baseball.

Introduce the Book

PICTURE WALK As you share the title and cover, ask children what game they think this story is about. Have children pantomime some baseball actions, such as pitching, catching, throwing. Ask children to preview the illustrations and tell what the characters are doing. Then have them read the book to find out who can play ball. **PREDICT/SET PURPOSE**

Guided Reading

Page 2 **FOCUS STRATEGY** *Use Picture Clues to Confirm Meaning* Readers can use pictures to confirm words as they read. You can use these prompts to confirm the reading.

Look at the picture. What is this animal? What is it doing? Now read the sentence. Does it match the picture?

Page 6 **FOCUS STRATEGY** *Self-Correct* Readers who misread a word will often realize that it does not make sense and will correct the error on their own. Use the following prompts to call attention to and reinforce this behavior.

At first you said ＿＿. Then you changed it to ＿＿. What did you notice that helped you change your mind?

Monitor Comprehension

1. **Are these animals real or make-believe? How can you tell?** *(They are make-believe. They are wearing clothes and playing baseball as people do.)* **CRITICAL: DISTINGUISH BETWEEN FANTASY AND REALITY**

2. **Read page 8 again. What happens on this page that is important?** *(Possible response: Everyone gets to play.)* **CRITICAL: EXPRESS PERSONAL OPINIONS**

3. **What other games do you think these animals might play?** *(Responses will vary.)* **INFERENTIAL: SPECULATE**

Write in Response to Reading

Talk with children about other games they can play. Choose a favorite game as a group, and discuss actions that children do to play the game. List the action words on the board. Then have children illustrate an action and complete the sentence frames *Who will ＿＿ here? ＿＿ will ＿＿!*

VOCABULARY LIST

found

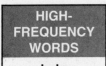

HIGH-FREQUENCY WORDS

help

these

who

Lost and Found

by Anne W. Phillips

Summary

The sheep have lost Bo Peep and no one will help find her.

Introduce the Book

PICTURE WALK Read aloud or recite with children the nursery rhyme about Little Bo Peep. Then share the title and cover illustration. Ask what this story is about, and have children tell what clues in the title and the illustration helped them decide. Then have them preview the illustrations and tell what the characters are doing. Have children read to find out how Bo Peep and her sheep find each other. **PREDICT/SET PURPOSE**

Guided Reading

Page 2 **FOCUS STRATEGY** *Use Context Clues to Confirm Meaning* Readers can use context to confirm unfamiliar words. Use the following prompts to help children use context to confirm words.

You said ____. Does that make sense? Read the rest of the sentence. What word would make sense here?

Page 5 **FOCUS STRATEGY** *Look for Words You Know* Readers can use similar words they know to help them identify new words. Use the following prompts to help children use this strategy.

What word do you know that looks like this? How does it sound? Now change the beginning sound. What is this word?

Monitor Comprehension

1. **Why didn't the other animals help the sheep?** *(They were all too busy.)* **LITERAL: NOTE DETAILS**

2. **How did the sheep find Bo Peep?** *(They went to the Lost and Found.)* **INFERENTIAL: IMPORTANT DETAILS**

3. **How is this story like the nursery rhyme "Little Bo Peep"? How is it different?** *(Both have the same characters. In this story Bo Peep is lost. In the nursery rhyme the sheep are lost.)* **INFERENTIAL: COMPARE AND CONTRAST**

Write in Response to Reading

Help children think of other animals the sheep might have asked to help and excuses these animals might have given. Then have children illustrate an animal and complete the sentence frames *"Not me," said the ____. "I'm __ __."*

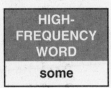

Red

by Catherine James

Summary

Everyone thinks Red the cat is looking fat, but they are in for a big surprise!

Introduce the Book

PICTURE WALK Show the cover and read the title. Explain that Red is the cat. Then have children preview the illustrations. Ask them to tell who is talking to Red and what she is doing. Have them read the book to find out where Red is going. **PREDICT/SET PURPOSE**

Guided Reading

Page 2 **FOCUS STRATEGY** *Self-Correct* When a reader misreads a word, he or she may quickly correct the mistake. Use the following prompts to affirm a child's correction.

You said ____. Then you changed it to ____. How did you know that you needed to change the word? How did you know that the new word was correct?

Page 6 **FOCUS STRATEGY** *Use Picture Clues to Confirm Meaning* Readers can use clues from the pictures to identify unfamiliar words. Use the following prompts to confirm children are using this strategy.

What time of day is it? What is happening? Why do you think she is looking for the cat? Now remember to think about the picture as you read the sentences.

Monitor Comprehension

1. **Why do you think Mrs. Bensen got up to look for Red?** (*Possible response: Mrs. Bensen was worried because Red did not come home.*) **CRITICAL: INTERPRET CHARACTERS' MOTIVATIONS**

2. **How did Red surprise Mrs. Bensen?** (*She had kittens.*) **INFERENTIAL: DRAW CONCLUSIONS**

3. **How do you think Mrs. Bensen will feel about the new kittens?** (*Responses will vary.*) **CRITICAL: SPECULATE**

Write in Response to Reading

Invite children to draw pictures of cats, real or imaginary. Then ask them to write a description of the cat they drew.

What's Up?

by Mary Louise Bourget

Summary

Two children discuss what they see in the sky, both at night and during the day.

Introduce the Book

PICTURE WALK Show the cover and read the title. Have children point up. Then discuss the meaning of the phrase *What's up?* as a way of asking what is going on. Then have children preview the illustrations and tell about what the children are doing. Ask them to read the book to find out what is up. **PREDICT/SET PURPOSE**

Guided Reading

Pages 4–5 **FOCUS STRATEGY** *Use Picture Clues to Confirm Meaning* Readers can use the illustrations to confirm what they read. Use the following prompts to confirm this strategy.

Look at the picture. What things can you see in the sky? Can you find the word that names each thing you see in the sky?

Pages 6–7 **FOCUS STRATEGY** *Look for Word Bits and Parts* Readers having difficulty with a long word can look for small words or parts of the word that they can read. Use the following prompts to encourage using this strategy.

Look at the letters in the word. Can you find a small word that you can read? Can you find a group of letters that you can read? Put the parts you can read together. What do you think the word is? Does it make sense in the sentence?

Monitor Comprehension

1. **What can be seen in the daytime sky?** *(the sun, clouds, birds, kites, and balloons)* **LITERAL: NOTE DETAILS**

2. **What can be seen in the nighttime sky?** *(the moon, stars, bats, bugs, and airplanes)* **LITERAL: NOTE DETAILS**

3. **What does the child mean when he asks *What's up?* at the end of the story?** *(Possible response: He is asking what the other boy is doing.)* **INFERENTIAL: DRAW CONCLUSIONS**

Write in Response to Reading

Brainstorm with children a list of location words, such as *down, in, out, over, under.* Have children choose a location word to complete the question *What's ____?* Then have them illustrate and write an answer.

The Little Chicks Sing

retold by Miryam Acevedo-Bouchard and Kathryn Corbett

Summary

This is a retelling of "los pollitos dicen," a traditional Latin American children's song about little chicks that ask their mother for constant attention.

Introduce the Book

PICTURE WALK Show the cover and read the title. Have children preview the illustrations and tell what the chicks might want from their mother. Point out the words *peep*, *peep*, and *pio*, and help children pronounce *pio* (pē′ō). Explain that this story is a song that is sung by children in Latin America. Then have children read to find out what the mother does for her chicks. **PREDICT/SET PURPOSE**

Guided Reading

Page 3 **FOCUS STRATEGY** *Read Ahead* Readers can often figure out a difficult word by reading ahead, and then using the text to decide what word makes sense. Use the following prompts to encourage this strategy.

Keep reading. What do the chicks want? What do you think that tricky word was? Use your word in the sentence. Does it make sense?

Page 6 **FOCUS STRATEGY** *Use Picture Clues to Confirm Meaning* Readers can use the pictures to confirm the reading of a passage. Use the following prompts to encourage using this strategy.

Look at the picture. Where are the chicks and what are they doing? Now look for those words as you read.

Monitor Comprehension

1. **What do the chicks need from their mother?** *(They need food and to be kept warm.)* **INFERENTIAL: SUMMARIZE**

2. **How does the hen take care of her chicks?** *(She gives them corn and protects them with her wings while they sleep.)* **INFERENTIAL: SUMMARIZE**

3. **What do you think will happen next?** *(Responses will vary.)* **INFERENTIAL: SPECULATE**

Write in Response to Reading

Brainstorm with children other baby animals and what they might need from their parents. Then have children illustrate a baby animal and write what it might ask of its mother or father.

Look What I Can Read!

by Anne W. Phillips

Summary

A girl discovers the joys of reading different things in different places.

Introduce the Book

PICTURE WALK As you share the title and cover, discuss with children the kinds of things they like to read. Have children look through the pictures and tell what the girl is reading. Then have children read to find out how the girl feels about reading. **PREDICT/SET PURPOSE**

Guided Reading

Page 3 **FOCUS STRATEGY** *Use Picture Clues to Confirm Meaning* Readers can use the illustrations to confirm words. Use the following prompts to encourage this strategy.

The first sentence told what the girl can read and where. What is she reading here? Where is she?

Page 6 **FOCUS STRATEGY** *Look for Word Bits and Parts* When an unfamiliar word is long, readers can often find parts of the word that they can read. Use the following prompts to encourage using this strategy.

Look at the word. Now cover parts of it with your fingers. Can you find any parts of the word that you can read? Put those parts together and try the word. Does your word make sense in the sentence?

Monitor Comprehension

1. **What are some things the girl can read?** *(stories, magazines, letters, comics, directions, and books)* **INFERENTIAL: SUMMARIZE**

2. **How do you think the girl feels about reading? How can you tell?** *(Possible response: She likes to read. She is smiling when she is reading, and she reads so many different things.)* **INFERENTIAL: DETERMINE CHARACTERS' EMOTIONS**

3. **What kinds of things do you like to read?** *(Responses will vary.)* **CRITICAL: EXPRESS PERSONAL OPINIONS**

Write in Response to Reading

Invite children to write more pages for the book. Have them brainstorm other items that they can read, such as menus, recipes, calendars, and signs. Children can illustrate their pages and write text by completing the sentence *I can read* ____. Remind them to tell both what they can read and where they might read it.

VOCABULARY
LIST

danced

king's

HIGH-
FREQUENCY
WORDS

outside

town

The King Who Loved to Dance

by Gail Tuchman

Summary

A king loves to dance to a singer's song but becomes sad when the singer goes away. The village animals provide a solution.

Introduce the Book

PICTURE WALK Read aloud the title and share the story illustrations with children. Ask them to describe what they see in each picture. In discussing the illustrations, use the story vocabulary that may be unfamiliar, such as *slope, neighed,* and *brayed.* Point out the way the characters are dressed and the story setting. **PREDICT/SET PURPOSE**

Guided Reading

Page 4   **FOCUS STRATEGY** *Use Picture Clues to Confirm Meaning* Readers often need to use the picture to confirm a word they have read. Use the following prompts to coach the reader in the reading of *slope.*

You said *slip.* Does that make sense? Look at the picture. Do you remember where the king was dancing before? Where is he now? Do you remember the word I used when we were talking about the king on this page?

Page 8   **FOCUS STRATEGY** *Reread Aloud* When a reader pauses because of a challenge, having the child reread aloud reinforces what was read and gives support for the unknown word.

That's a tricky word. What do you see at the beginning? Do you see any part of the word you know? Read that part of the sentence again. Think about what would make sense. Try your word.

Monitor Comprehension

1. **Where did the king dance first?** *(into town)* **LITERAL: SEQUENCE**

2. **What do you think made the king happy?** *(dancing)* **INFERENTIAL: CAUSE-EFFECT**

3. **What might this story be like if the king loved to sleep?** *(Responses will vary.)* **CRITICAL: AUTHOR'S CRAFT**

Write in Response to Reading

Have children write a story about something they love to do. Have them model their story after the sentence structures in *The King Who Loved to Dance* and title it *The Boy Who Loved to* ____ or *The Girl Who Loved to* ____ .

The Night Walk

by Jennifer Jacobson

Summary

A girl finds little creatures as she explores her backyard at night.

Introduce the Book

PICTURE WALK As you share the title and cover, discuss with children the kinds of things they think they might see on a walk at night. Have children look through the pictures and name the animals the girl sees. Then have children read to find out what special friend the girl finds in her yard. **PREDICT/SET PURPOSE**

Guided Reading

Page 3 **FOCUS STRATEGY** *Use Picture Clues to Confirm Meaning* Readers understand that the text should match the illustrations. Use the following prompts to confirm children's use of the illustrations.

Look at the picture. What does the girl see? The words you read told about this picture. I like the way you pay close attention to the pictures as you read.

Page 7 **FOCUS STRATEGY** *Make Predictions* Readers can use hints in the text and in the pictures to predict what may happen in a story. Use the following prompts to help children predict what may happen next.

Read the sentences. Now we know this is not one of the other animals. Look at the picture. What kind of animal do you think is under the rock? What do you think the girl will do?

Monitor Comprehension

1. **What happened on the girl's night walk?** (*She found a toad, a bug, a moth, and a lizard. She took the lizard inside to keep as a pet.*)
   INFERENTIAL: SUMMARIZE

2. **What do you think the girl was looking for?** (*Possible response: a pet*)
   INFERENTIAL: DRAW CONCLUSIONS

3. **Which of the animals would you like to keep?** (*Responses will vary.*)
   CRITICAL: EXPRESS PERSONAL OPINIONS

Write in Response to Reading

Invite children to think about other animals they might find outside. Encourage them to think about the way each animal looks and what it does. Then have them draw an animal and write about it using the story pattern: *It's a _____. A ___ .*

My Wild Woolly

by Deborah Eaton

Summary

A boy has an imaginary friend that can do everything he does.

Introduce the Book

PICTURE WALK As you share the title and cover, discuss what children think the Wild Woolly is. Then, as they preview the pictures, discuss what the boy and the Wild Woolly are doing. Have children read to find out what kind of creature the Wild Woolly is. **PREDICT/SET PURPOSE**

Guided Reading

Page 3 **FOCUS STRATEGY** *Use Context Clues to Confirm Meaning* Readers understand that the text should always make sense. Use the following prompts to confirm children's use of context clues.

You said ____. Does that make sense? What do you think would make sense in the sentence? Now try your new word. Does it make sense?

Page 7 **FOCUS STRATEGY** *Self-Correct* Use the following prompts to affirm children who correct their own errors.

At first you said ____. Then you changed it to ____. What clues told you that you needed to make a change?

Monitor Comprehension

1. **Why do you think the boy's mom can't see the Wild Woolly?** *(Responses will vary.)* **CRITICAL: EXPRESS PERSONAL OPINIONS**

2. **Do you think this is a real story or a make-believe story? Why?** *(Possible response: This is a make-believe story. The Wild Woolly is make-believe.)* **CRITICAL: DISTINGUISH BETWEEN FANTASY AND REALITY**

3. **What happened at the beginning, the middle, and the end of this story?** *(In the beginning the boy saw the Wild Woolly outside, and then he and the Wild Woolly played. At the end, the Wild Woolly slept under the boy's bed.)* **INFERENTIAL: SUMMARIZE**

Write in Response to Reading

Invite children to look back at the Wild Woolly and to tell whether or not they think this creature matches its name. Then work with children to brainstorm a list of other imaginary creatures, such as Big Fuzzy or Soft Snuggly. Have them draw an imaginary creature, give it a name, and write a sentence about it.

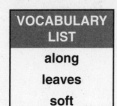

VOCABULARY LIST

along

leaves

soft

How 100 Dandelions Grew

by Louisa Ernesto

Summary

One dandelion seed grows a flower that in turn produces 100 little seeds that scatter.

Introduce the Book

PICTURE WALK Share the title and cover with children. Have them preview the pictures and tell what they think is happening on the pages. Have children read to find out how dandelions grow. **PREDICT/SET PURPOSE**

Guided Reading

Pages 2–3   **FOCUS STRATEGY** *Use Picture Clues to Confirm Meaning* Readers know that they can use the pictures to understand the text. Use the following prompts to confirm children's use of picture clues.

You looked at the picture and said ＿＿. What part of the picture helped you read the words? I like the way you used the picture clues.

Page 7   **FOCUS STRATEGY** *Self-Correct* When a reader misreads a word, he or she will often catch the mistake and correct it without help. Use the following prompts to encourage children to correct their own errors.

Something wasn't quite right. Try reading it again. That time you changed it to ＿＿. What clues told you how to change it?

Monitor Comprehension

1. **What happened when the seed "went riding on the wind"?** *(Possible response: The wind carried it up into the air.)* **INFERENTIAL: DRAW CONCLUSIONS**

2. **Do you think this is a real story or a make-believe story? Why?** *(Possible response: This is a real story because it tells about the way dandelions really grow.)* **CRITICAL: DISTINGUISH BETWEEN FANTASY AND REALITY**

3. **What do you think will happen to the dandelion seeds flying through the air?** *(Possible response: The seeds will land and grow into new dandelions.)* **CRITICAL: INTERPRET TEXT STRUCTURE**

Write in Response to Reading

Invite children to write science facts on index cards. They may choose to tell how another kind of seed travels or an interesting fact they know about an animal. Place the cards in a container or on a ring, and have children work in pairs to play a question-and-answer game with the cards.

Green Green Green

retold by Ruby Mae

Summary

This rhyme celebrates the colors that brighten our world.

Introduce the Book

PICTURE WALK As you share the title, discuss what is green on the cover. Then have children name other colors on the cover. Have children preview the pictures and name the animals. Have children read to find out what the animals say about the colors. **PREDICT/SET PURPOSE**

Guided Reading

Page 2 **FOCUS STRATEGY** *Look for Word Bits and Parts* The following prompts will help to encourage children to find parts that they can read in words.

That is a long word. Look at all the letters. Can you see any parts of the word that you can read? Read the parts you know.

Page 6 **FOCUS STRATEGY** *Use Picture Clues to Confirm Meaning* Use the following prompts to affirm the use of picture clues.

Look at the picture. What is the bird doing? Do the words and the picture go together? Do the words tell about the picture?

Monitor Comprehension

1. **How are all these pages alike? How are they different?** *(They are alike because they all tell about a color and an animal. They are different because they all tell about a different color and a different animal.)*
    INFERENTIAL: COMPARE AND CONTRAST

2. **Look at pages 3 and 5. Can you find a hint the artist gave to let you know what color would be next?** *(the yellow flower on page 3; the piece of the purple kite on page 5)* **LITERAL: NOTE DETAILS**

3. **Which is your favorite picture? Tell why you like it.** *(Responses will vary.)* **CRITICAL: EXPRESS PERSONAL OPINIONS**

Write in Response to Reading

Have children choose a favorite color and write a sentence telling about something that is that color. They might use a marker of the color to write and illustrate the sentence.

The Green Grass Grows All Around

retold by Ruby Mae

Summary

The traditional folk song is retold in an urban setting.

Introduce the Book

PICTURE WALK Share the title and tell children that the words in this book are from a song. Have children preview the pictures and tell where they think this story takes place. Have children read to find out what grows with the green grass. **PREDICT/SET PURPOSE**

Guided Reading

Page 2 **FOCUS STRATEGY** *Look for Words You Know* Readers can use similar words they know to identify a new word. The following prompts will help you confirm children's identification of similar words.

Look at the word. Can you see any other words on the page that look like this? Words that look a lot alike usually sound alike. Now try this word.

Page 7 **FOCUS STRATEGY** *Use Picture Clues to Confirm Meaning* Readers can use the pictures to confirm what they read. Use the following prompts to affirm the use of picture clues.

What do you see in the picture? Can you find its name on the page? Do the words tell about this picture? How can pictures help you read?

Monitor Comprehension

1. **A song often has words that repeat. What words repeat on each page of this book?** *(The green grass grows all around, all around, And the green grass grows all around.)* **LITERAL: NOTE DETAILS**

2. **What other things might be added to this story?** *(Responses will vary.)* **CRITICAL: EXPRESS PERSONAL OPINIONS**

3. **What are some other songs that keep adding new words with each verse?** *(Possible responses: "Old MacDonald," "I Know an Old Lady," and "Fiddle-I-Fee")* **CRITICAL: INTERPRET TEXT STRUCTURE**

Write in Response to Reading

Have children write about something they might find in a backyard. They can write about their own yard or an imaginary one. You may want to have children brainstorm items and then pick one. Children can begin their stories with the words *In my backyard there is* ____.

Slowpoke Snail

by Y. Kim Choi

Summary

Here is a playful explanation of how a snail protects itself.

Introduce the Book

PICTURE WALK Name some animals, such as a porcupine and a skunk, and ask how the animals protect themselves. Then display the cover and read the title. Ask whether a snail might need to protect itself. Have children preview the pictures and name the animals they see. Then have children read to find out how a snail protects itself. **PREDICT/SET PURPOSE**

Guided Reading

Page 3 **FOCUS STRATEGY** *Use Context Clues to Confirm Meaning* Readers can use the context of a sentence or passage to confirm a word. The following prompts will help confirm children's use of context to identify words.

Read the sentence again. Can you think of a word that would make sense in the sentence? Look at the beginning and ending sounds of this word. Do you know a word that begins and ends like this that would make sense here?

Page 5 **FOCUS STRATEGY** *Use Picture Clues to Confirm Meaning* Readers often use the pictures to confirm what they read. Use the following prompts to confirm the use of picture clues.

What do you see in the picture? Do the words tell about what is happening in this picture? I like the way you know that the picture should match the words.

Monitor Comprehension

1. **What animals might try to eat a snail?** *(a bird and a fish)* **LITERAL: NOTE DETAILS**

2. **Why doesn't a snail have to be fast?** *(A snail has a hard shell for protection.)* **INFERENTIAL: DRAW CONCLUSIONS**

3. **Why do you think birds, fish, and frogs move fast?** *(Possible response: These animals do not have shells to protect them so they have to run away from other animals.)* **INFERENTIAL: DRAW CONCLUSIONS**

Write in Response to Reading

Discuss with children other animals they know and ways these animals protect themselves. Have children select an animal and write a sentence telling how the animal protects itself. Ask them to illustrate their sentences.

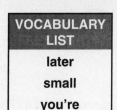
VOCABULARY
LIST

later

small

you're

Skimper-Scamper

by Jeff Newell

Summary

Lisa draws animals that run off the paper and create a big mess.

Introduce the Book

PICTURE WALK Share the title and cover illustration with children. As children preview the illustrations, use the expression *skimper-scamper* to describe the movements of the animals. Suggest that children read the story to find out what the girl and the animals do. **PREDICT/SET PURPOSE**

Guided Reading

Pages 4–5 **FOCUS STRATEGY** *Use Picture Clues to Confirm Meaning* The following prompts will help affirm children's use of pictures to identify words.

Look at the picture. Does the picture match the words you read?

Page 10 **FOCUS STRATEGY** *Use Context Clues to Confirm Meaning* The following prompts will help affirm children's use of context clues.

Read the sentence again. What would make sense here?

Page 13 **FOCUS STRATEGY** *Reread Aloud* The following prompts will help you guide children's rereading of a passage for understanding and expression.

Now we know what Lisa said. How do you think she sounds? Reread the sentences and try to make them sound as Lisa might sound.

Monitor Comprehension

1. **Why did Lisa draw the cat and then the dog?** *(She wanted the cat to get rid of the mouse; then she wanted the dog to get rid of the cat.)* **INFERENTIAL: CAUSE-EFFECT**

2. **Why did Lisa make an airplane?** *(She promised the animals a ride in her plane if they would clean up.)* **INFERENTIAL: DRAW CONCLUSIONS**

3. **Do you think Lisa will draw more animals? Why?** *(Responses will vary.)* **CRITICAL: SPECULATE**

Write in Response to Reading

Discuss with children animals they might draw at school and what the animals might do if they ran off the paper in your classroom. Have children draw an animal and write about what it might do if it could *skimper-scamper* off the paper.

Today Is Monday

retold by Ruby Mae

Summary

Through the pattern of a traditional song, the days of the week are enumerated with an activity for each day.

Introduce the Book

PICTURE WALK Share the title and cover illustration with children. Discuss the activities on the cover and count them. Have children predict what the book will show. **PREDICT/SET PURPOSE**

Guided Reading

Page 2 **FOCUS STRATEGY** *Use Picture Clues to Confirm Meaning* The following prompts will help encourage children's use of pictures.

Look at the picture. What are the children doing? The words tell about the day and what the children do on that day. Can you find the words that match the picture? The picture can help you make sense of the words.

Page 4 **FOCUS STRATEGY** *Make Predictions* When a text has a repeating pattern, readers can use the pattern to predict and to confirm what they read. The following prompts will help affirm children's use of context for predicting words.

Read these sentences again. How are these words like the words on pages 2 and 3? How are they different? What words do you think will change on the next page? Can you predict what the next page will tell?

Monitor Comprehension

1. **What activities do the children do at school?** (*art, playing in snow, music, sharing, having a birthday party*) **INFERENTIAL: SUMMARIZE**

2. **Where are the children playing on Saturday? How can you tell?** (*They are in a park because there is a path, playground equipment, trees, and a park bench.*) **INFERENTIAL: DRAW CONCLUSIONS**

3. **Which day in the book would be your favorite? Why?** (*Responses will vary.*) **CRITICAL: EXPRESS PERSONAL OPINIONS**

Write in Response to Reading

Have children choose a day of the week and draw and write about something your class does on that day. They should use the story pattern from the book.

If You Were a Bat

by Susan McCloskey

Summary

Facts about bats are presented through a boy's imaginings.

Introduce the Book

PICTURE WALK Share the title and cover with children. Discuss what the boy is wearing and why he has on these things. As children look through the pages, discuss what the bats and the boy are doing. Have children read to find out information about bats. **PREDICT/SET PURPOSE**

Guided Reading

Page 2 **FOCUS STRATEGY** *Use Context Clues to Confirm Meaning* The following prompts will help encourage children to use context to identify words.

Skip the tricky word and read the rest of the sentence. Can you think of a word that might make sense in this sentence? Put your word in and read the sentence again.

Page 6 **FOCUS STRATEGY** *Use Picture Clues to Confirm Meaning* Readers know they can look at the picture and use what they see to confirm the words. Use these prompts to confirm the use of picture clues.

Look at the picture. Can you tell what the bat is doing? Look at the words. Now can you tell me what the bat is doing? The words and the picture work together to make the meaning clear.

Monitor Comprehension

1. **What did this story tell you about bats?** *(Bats fly around at night; they eat bugs; they lick their fur to keep it clean; they sleep all day.)* **INFERENTIAL: SUMMARIZE**

2. **How do you think the boy feels about eating bugs? How can you tell?** *(Possible response: He would not like to eat bugs because he looks afraid to eat the bug on the page.)* **INFERENTIAL: DRAW CONCLUSIONS**

3. **Does this book tell about real bats or make-believe bats?** *(The pictures show drawings of make-believe bats, but the information is true about real bats.)* **CRITICAL: DISTINGUISH BETWEEN FANTASY AND REALITY**

Write in Response to Reading

Work with children to brainstorm a list of wild animals they know. Ask them to tell one fact about each animal they suggest. Then have them choose an animal and complete the sentence frame *If you were a _____ you would _____.*

Hare's Big Tug-of-War

retold by Cheyenne Cisco

Summary

In this retelling of an African fable, Hare gets even with Elephant and Hippo for eating his vegetables.

Introduce the Book

PICTURE WALK Share the title and cover illustration with children. As children look through the pages, discuss what the animals are doing. Then have them read to discover how the hare has a tug-of-war. **PREDICT/SET PURPOSE**

Guided Reading

Page 2 **FOCUS STRATEGY** *Use Context Clues to Confirm Meaning* The following prompts will help encourage children to use context to identify words.

You said ____. Does that make sense? Can you think of a word that might make sense in this sentence?

Page 7 **FOCUS STRATEGY** *Self-Correct* Readers will notice when a sentence or passage does not make sense and will often correct the word that caused an interruption in meaning on their own. Use the following prompts.

You said ____. Then you changed it to ____. Why did you change it?

Monitor Comprehension

1. **What was Hare's problem?** *(He didn't want Elephant and Hippo to eat all his vegetables.)* **INFERENTIAL: SUMMARIZE**

2. **Who did Elephant and Hippo think they were having a tug-of-war with when they were pulling on the rope?** *(They thought they were tugging with Hare.)* **INFERENTIAL: DRAW CONCLUSIONS**

3. **What do you think will happen the next time Elephant and Hippo try to eat Hare's vegetables?** *(Possible response: They will stop when Hare tells them to because he won the tug-of-war.)* **CRITICAL: INTERPRET STORY EVENTS**

Write in Response to Reading

Invite children to suggest what Elephant or Hippo may have said when Hare won the tug-of-war. Have them illustrate one of the animals and write, perhaps using a speech balloon, what the animal may have said.

VOCABULARY LIST

shadow

trapped

Davy Crockett and the Wild Cat

by Sharon Fear

Summary

In this tall tale, the legendary Davy Crockett tames a wild cat.

Introduce the Book

PICTURE WALK Explain that as people told stories about Davy Crockett, the stories became more and more exaggerated. Then share the title and cover of the story. As children look through the pictures, point out exaggerations. Have children read to find out what happens when Davy Crockett meets a wild cat. **PREDICT/SET PURPOSE**

Guided Reading

Page 2 **FOCUS STRATEGY** *Reread Aloud* When a piece of text has been read, rereading that same text aloud can help confirm meaning. Use the following prompts.

Look at the mark at the end of the first sentence. How do you think that sentence would sound if someone were telling this story? Reread it aloud and try to sound as if you were a storyteller.

Page 6 **FOCUS STRATEGY** *Look for Word Bits and Parts* Use the following prompts to help children look for parts in a longer word.

Move your finger along the word, and see if you can find any parts you can read. Say the parts you can read, and then put them together.

Monitor Comprehension

1. **How do you know that Davy Crockett was strong?** *(He could run like a deer, swim like a fish, and hold a bear.)* **INFERENTIAL: DRAW CONCLUSIONS**

2. **How did Davy Crockett tame the wild cat?** *(He had bigger teeth and could howl louder than the wild cat.)* **INFERENTIAL: SUMMARIZE**

3. **What do you think might happen if Davy Crockett met an alligator?** *(Possible response: He might tame it.)* **CRITICAL: SPECULATE**

Write in Response to Reading

Write on the board the sentence *He was as fast as a deer.* Explain that Davy Crockett was being compared to a deer. Ask children to name other animals and to tell a characteristic of each, such as *monkeys are silly.* Then have them write and illustrate a sentence that compares an imaginary hero to an animal.

Every Cat

by Anne W. Phillips

Summary

All cats need love and attention from the people who care for them.

Introduce the Book

PICTURE WALK Ask children to tell what they know about the things a pet needs. Then share the title and cover illustration. Ask what children think cats need. Have children preview the pages and tell what people are doing for the cats. Have children read to find out what every cat needs. **PREDICT/SET PURPOSE**

Guided Reading

Page 3 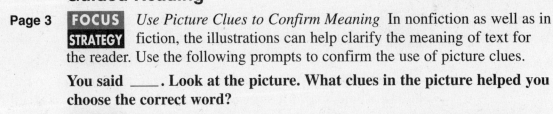 *Use Picture Clues to Confirm Meaning* In nonfiction as well as in fiction, the illustrations can help clarify the meaning of text for the reader. Use the following prompts to confirm the use of picture clues.

You said ____. Look at the picture. What clues in the picture helped you choose the correct word?

Page 9 **FOCUS STRATEGY** *Self-Correct* Readers who misread a word will notice that the passage does not make sense with the wrong word. Children will often correct themselves to make the passage make sense. Use the following prompts to help children correct words they misread.

You said ____. Then you changed the word to ____. Did the sentence make sense with the first word? Does it make sense now? I like the way you changed the word when you knew the sentence did not make sense.

Monitor Comprehension

1. **What are some things that every cat needs?** *(Possible responses: a friend to feed it, let the sun in, help it, and let it in; a toy; a shadow; a bed; a lap; someone special)* **INFERENTIAL: RETELL**

2. **Why do you think the author wrote this book?** *(to tell people how to take care of cats)* **CRITICAL: RECOGNIZE AUTHOR'S PURPOSE**

3. **Would you like to have a cat for a pet? Why or why not?** *(Responses will vary.)* **CRITICAL: EXPRESS PERSONAL OPINIONS**

Write in Response to Reading

Ask children to think about their own pet, or about a pet they would like to have. Have them complete the sentence frame *Every ____ needs a ____* to tell about the pet. Then have them illustrate their sentences.

Plenty of Pets

by Rosie Benson

Summary

Each day Mom, who is a veterinarian, brings home pets that need homes.

Introduce the Book

PICTURE WALK Share the title and cover illustration. Tell children that the mother in the story is a veterinarian, and ask what a veterinarian, or vet, does for animals. Have children preview the pictures and tell what they see happening. Then ask them to read to find out what this family does for all its pets. **PREDICT/SET PURPOSE**

Guided Reading

Page 6 **FOCUS STRATEGY** *Use Picture Clues to Confirm Meaning* Use the following prompts to help children confirm that the pictures match the words.

Look at the picture. What is the girl doing? Do the words tell about the picture? It's good that you know that the words should make sense and tell about the picture.

Page 9 **FOCUS STRATEGY** *Make Predictions* Readers can use story patterns and what they know to predict what might happen next. Use the following prompts to encourage children to make and confirm predictions as they read.

On Tuesday Mom had two animals. This is Wednesday and Mom has three animals. What do you think will come next? Let's see if the predictions are correct as we keep reading.

Monitor Comprehension

1. **What did all the pets need?** *(new homes)* **LITERAL: NOTE DETAILS**

2. **How can you tell that this girl likes animals?** *(Possible response: She was happy to get the animals and she took good care of them.)* **METACOGNITIVE: DETERMINE CHARACTERS' TRAITS**

3. **Why do you think the family did not keep the pets?** *(Possible response: There were just too many pets.)* **CRITICAL: EXPRESS PERSONAL OPINIONS**

Write in Response to Reading

Ask children to write and illustrate their own number sentences about animals. Have them choose three kinds of animals and write and illustrate a sentence about one animal, then about two animals, and then about three animals. Encourage them to think about the funny things each animal might do.

Pet Day

by Lois Bick

Summary

On Pet Day, every pet wins a prize. But what if you don't have a pet? A girl very creatively finds a prize-winning pet.

Introduce the Book

PICTURE WALK Share the title and cover illustration. Discuss what children think Pet Day is. Then have children preview the pictures and name the pets they see. Ask them to read to find out what kind of pet the girl brings for Pet Day. **PREDICT/SET PURPOSE**

Guided Reading

Page 4 **FOCUS STRATEGY** *Use Picture Clues to Confirm Meaning* Readers know that the pictures in the story match the text. Use the following prompts to encourage children to make sure that the pictures match the words.

You said ____. Does that make sense? Does it match the picture? I'm glad that you know that the words should tell about the picture.

Page 7 **FOCUS STRATEGY** *Look for Word Bits and Parts* Readers can find readable parts in unfamiliar words. The parts can help the reader identify the word. Use the following prompts to encourage children to look for readable parts of unfamiliar words as they read.

That's a long word. Can you find any parts of the word that you can read? Are there any small words you know in this word? Say the parts you can read. Do you know any word that has those parts and would make sense here?

Monitor Comprehension

1. **Why did the girl want a pet?** *(She wanted to have a pet to bring to school for Pet Day.)* **INFERENTIAL: DRAW CONCLUSIONS**

2. **How did the girl get a pet to take to school?** *(She caught grasshoppers outside.)* **LITERAL: NOTE DETAILS**

3. **What do you think the girl will do with her pets after Pet Day?** *(Possible response: She will let them go.)* **CRITICAL: SPECULATE**

Write in Response to Reading

Ask children to think about their own pet or a pet they might like to have. Have them illustrate the pet and create a prize for the pet to win. Then ask them to write a sentence about the pet and its prize.

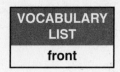
How to Make a Lion Mask

by Hannah Markley

Summary

This is a how-to book that gives directions for making a lion mask.

Introduce the Book

PICTURE WALK Share the title and cover illustration. Discuss what children think they will learn in this book. Then have children preview the pictures. Ask them to identify the materials they see. Then have them read to find out how to make a lion mask. **PREDICT/SET PURPOSE**

Guided Reading

Page 4 **FOCUS STRATEGY** *Use Context Clues to Confirm Meaning* The context of a sentence can help a reader figure out an unfamiliar word. Use the following prompts to encourage children to use context to figure out a word.

That's a tricky word. What word do you think belongs here? Read the rest of the sentence. Now can you figure out what this word is? Try the sentence with your word. Does it make sense?

Page 10 **FOCUS STRATEGY** *Look for Word Bits and Parts* Readers can look at unfamiliar words to find small parts of the word that they can read. The parts can help the reader identify the word. Use the following prompts to encourage children to look for readable parts of unfamiliar words as they read.

That's a long word. Can you find any parts of the word that you can read? Are there any small words you know in this word? Put the parts together. What do you think this word is?

Monitor Comprehension

1. **What things can you use to make a lion mask?** *(paper, scissors, glue, crayons, markers, pencils, yarn, craft sticks)* **LITERAL: NOTE DETAILS**

2. **Tell how to make a lion mask.** *(Make a pattern, trace the pattern onto paper, cut out the mask shape, color and decorate it, and glue it on a stick.)* **INFERENTIAL: RETELL**

3. **What other animal masks might you make?** *(Responses will vary.)* **CRITICAL: SPECULATE**

Write in Response to Reading

As a group, write a series of directions for making a simple snack or craft. First have children make a list of the items needed. Then have them number the steps in the process. Encourage them to use the words *first, next,* and *last.*

Pet Riddles and Jokes with Franny and Frank

by Lisa Eisenberg

Summary

No silly pet tricks here—just a lot of fun with language play in jokes and riddles.

Introduce the Book

PICTURE WALK Read aloud the title of the book, and explain that the two characters tell the jokes and riddles in this book. Franny's lines are printed in pink, and Frank's are in blue. Discuss the pictures and the animals' actions in the book. Then have children read to learn some silly riddles and jokes. **PREDICT/SET PURPOSE**

Guided Reading

Page 2 **FOCUS STRATEGY** *Use Context Clues to Confirm Meaning* The context of a sentence can help a reader figure out an unfamiliar word. Use the following prompts to guide children in reading the word *sign*.

That's a tricky word. Look at the sentence again. It asks if you put up something. What might someone put up to find a missing dog?

Page 6 **FOCUS STRATEGY** *Look for Word Bits and Parts* Readers can often find small, readable parts in unfamiliar words. Use the following prompts to encourage children to look for readable parts in words.

That's a long word. Look at just the first three letters. Can you read this part? Are there any other parts of this word you can read? Put the parts together. What do you think this word is?

Monitor Comprehension

1. **The joke on page 2 is funny because Franny did not understand. What mistake did she make?** (*Franny thought the sign was for the dog.*) **INFERENTIAL: UNDERSTAND FIGURATIVE LANGUAGE**

2. **What did Franny want to do with birdseed?** (*She wanted to plant it to grow a bird.*) **LITERAL: NOTE DETAILS**

3. **Which riddle or joke did you like best?** (*Responses will vary.*) **CRITICAL: EXPRESS PERSONAL OPINIONS**

Write in Response to Reading

Encourage children to collect jokes and riddles for a group joke and riddle book. When the jokes and riddles have been written, help children read them aloud.

Lunch in Space

by Kana Riley

Summary

Learn how the astronauts prepare and clean up their meals in space.

Introduce the Book

PICTURE WALK Read aloud the title and share the cover with children. Have children look through the pictures and tell what seems to be different about preparing lunch in space. Then have children read to find out what is special about a space lunch. **PREDICT/SET PURPOSE**

Guided Reading

Page 5 **FOCUS STRATEGY** *Use Picture Clues to Confirm Meaning* Readers can tell from the actions illustrated in a picture what the words should say. Use the following prompts to confirm using pictures to understand the text.

When I think of floating, I think of something floating on water. What do the astronauts mean when they say something can float away? How does the picture help you?

Page 9 **FOCUS STRATEGY** *Self-Correct* Use the following prompts to encourage children to correct their own mistakes as they read.

You first said ____. Then you changed it to ____. Why did you change it?

Monitor Comprehension

1. **Why is lunch in space special?** *(Possible responses: Things can float away; foods come in special packages; you can sit on the wall or the ceiling to eat.)* **INFERENTIAL: RETELL**

2. **How is lunch in space like your lunch? How is it different?** *(Possible response: It is like lunch here because the astronauts eat some of the same things, they have to fix their food, and they have to clean up. It is different because they eat out of special trays, and they have to be careful so things don't float away.)* **INFERENTIAL: COMPARE AND CONTRAST**

3. **What is one thing you learned about space that you did not know before?** *(Responses will vary.)* **LITERAL: NOTE DETAILS**

Write in Response to Reading

Children can work in groups to develop a menu for a space breakfast or a space dinner. Remind them to consider how food should be contained to keep it from floating away. Using a sheet of construction paper, children can illustrate an astronaut's tray for the meal.

Alien Vacation

by F. R. Robinson

Summary

A family of aliens reviews the sights of Earth to see if they might enjoy
spending their vacation there.

Introduce the Book

PICTURE WALK Show the book and read aloud the title. Invite children to
think about where an alien might like to go for a vacation. Have children
preview the illustrations, stopping at page 15. Discuss what the aliens learn
about Earth. Then have children read to find out what the aliens do on their
vacation. **PREDICT/SET PURPOSE**

Guided Reading

Page 4   **FOCUS STRATEGY**   *Reread Aloud* Rereading passages aloud, particularly passages that
contain conversation, can help the reader make more sense of the
passages. The following prompts will encourage children to reread aloud.

**Look at the marks at the ends of the sentences. What do these tell you
about the way the alien says these words? Reread them aloud, and try to
make them sound the way you think the alien would sound.**

Page 9   **FOCUS STRATEGY**   *Make Predictions* Use the following prompts to encourage children
to make predictions as they read.

What do the aliens see? What do you think the aliens will say?

Monitor Comprehension

1. **What things did the aliens like about Earth? What things didn't they
   like?** *(They liked bugs, rocks, and the ocean. They did not like flowers or
   people.)* **INFERENTIAL: SUMMARIZE**

2. **Why do you think the aliens thought the people looked scary?** *(Possible
   response: They were so different from the aliens.)* **CRITICAL: INTERPRET
   CHARACTERS' MOTIVATIONS**

3. **What made the aliens decide to come to Earth?** *(They found creatures
   like themselves in the ocean.)* **INFERENTIAL: DRAW CONCLUSIONS**

Write in Response to Reading

Ask children to suggest places they like to visit. Make a list of the places and
discuss how the aliens might feel about each. Then have children illustrate an
alien visiting one of the places and write a speech balloon to show what the
alien might say.

How the Sky Got Its Stars

retold by Gail Tuchman

Summary

Based upon a Hopi legend, this story explains how Coyote help put the stars in the sky.

Introduce the Book

PICTURE WALK Read aloud the title, and tell children that this story is a legend told by the Hopi people. Explain that long ago, people would sometimes make up stories to explain why things happened. Have children look through the pictures and tell what they think is happening. Then have children read to find out how the legend says that stars got into the sky. **PREDICT/SET PURPOSE**

Guided Reading

Page 6   **FOCUS STRATEGY**   *Use Picture Clues to Confirm Meaning* Use the following prompts to have children use the picture clues to confirm meaning.

The words say that the animals made small, bright things. Look at the picture. What are the small, bright things the animals made? *(stars)*

Page 11   **FOCUS STRATEGY**   *Use Context Clues to Confirm Meaning* Use the following prompts to help children identify words in context.

You said ____ . Did that make sense? Read the sentence again. What word would make sense here? Does your word begin as this word does? Try your word in the sentence and see if it makes sense now.

Monitor Comprehension

1. **If you were one of the other animals, how would you feel about Coyote?** *(Possible responses: I would not like Coyote because he is lazy. I would want Coyote to help.)* **CRITICAL: IDENTIFY WITH CHARACTERS**

2. **How did Coyote accidentally do something good?** *(Coyote threw the stars up into the sky because he couldn't use them.)* **INFERENTIAL: SUMMARIZE**

3. **What do you think the animals said when they saw the stars up in the sky?** *(Responses will vary.)* **CRITICAL: SPECULATE**

Write in Response to Reading

Work with children to develop some questions about nature, such as *Why is grass green? How did fluffy clouds get in the sky? Why do flowers smell sweet?* Have them select a question and think of a possible answer for it. Then have them write and illustrate their questions and answers.

Let's Visit the Moon

by Ben Farrell

Summary

This nonfiction narrative playfully presents information about the moon.

Introduce the Book

PICTURE WALK Read aloud the title and show children the cover illustration. Explain that this book gives real information about the moon, but that the pictures show the information in a funny way. Have children look through the pictures and tell what is happening. Then have children read to find out what information about the moon is given. **PREDICT/SET PURPOSE**

Guided Reading

Page 6   **FOCUS STRATEGY**   *Use Picture Clues to Confirm Meaning* Use the following prompts to have children use the picture clues to confirm meaning.

What kind of space suits does the sentence tell about? How do you know what these space suits look like? How does the picture help you?

Page 10   **FOCUS STRATEGY**   *Self-Correct* The following prompts will reinforce children correcting themselves.

You said ____ . Then you changed it to ____ . Why did you change it? Good readers do that when something does not make sense.

Monitor Comprehension

1. **What parts of this book are real? What parts are make-believe?** *(The words give real information; the pictures show make-believe things happening.)* **CRITICAL: DISTINGUISH BETWEEN FANTASY AND REALITY**

2. **On page 11, it says that the moon has no living things. How does this explain why there is no food?** *(No food grows there; there is nothing there that needs to eat food.)* **CRITICAL: DRAW CONCLUSIONS**

3. **What did you learn about the moon that you did not know before?** *(Responses will vary.)* **LITERAL: NOTE DETAILS**

Write in Response to Reading

Have children draw a picture of their own spaceship and think about what they might need for a trip to the moon. On the back of the drawing, have children make a list of the things they would bring.

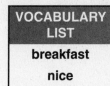
Dream Around the World

by Deborah Eaton

Summary

A boy's dream takes him on an adventure around the world.

Introduce the Book

PICTURE WALK Read aloud the title and ask children what they think might happen in this story. Have children look through the pictures and tell what is happening. Then have children read to find out what happens in the boy's dream. **PREDICT/SET PURPOSE**

Guided Reading

Page 2 **FOCUS STRATEGY** *Use Picture Clues to Confirm Meaning* Readers can often find information in pictures that makes the meaning of the text more clear. Use the following prompts to help children confirm that the pictures match the words.

Look at the pictures here. What do the swirling lines around the boy's head tell you? How does this picture go with the words? Look at the picture of the world. How does this picture go with the words?

Page 6 **FOCUS STRATEGY** *Read Ahead* When a word is difficult, readers can often read ahead and use the context of the rest of the passage to select the word that best completes the meaning. Use the following prompts to confirm using context to identify words.

You stopped. Go on and read the next part. Now what word do you think makes sense? Read the sentence again and put in your word.

Monitor Comprehension

1. **What did the boy dream about first, second, and third?** *(First he dreamed about eating with chopsticks, second he dreamed about playing with toy trucks, and third he dreamed about watching a baseball game.)* **LITERAL: SEQUENCE**

2. **When did the boy wake up? How can you tell?** *(He woke up when the sun came up. He is back home with his family.)* **CRITICAL: DRAW CONCLUSIONS**

3. **What do you think the boy told his family?** *(Responses will vary.)* **INFERENTIAL: SUMMARIZE**

Write in Response to Reading

Discuss with children other places they think the boy might have dreamed about. Have them choose a place and write and illustrate a sentence about it.

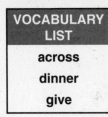

VOCABULARY LIST

across

dinner

give

Clean-Up Day

by Catherine James

Summary

The family works hard to clean up and get rid of the things they no longer need.

Introduce the Book

PICTURE WALK After you read the title and share the cover, discuss what might be done on a clean-up day at home. List children's responses on the board. Then have them look through the pictures to confirm some of their predictions. Then have children read to find out all this family does on clean-up day. **PREDICT/SET PURPOSE**

Guided Reading

Page 2 **FOCUS STRATEGY** *Look for Word Bits and Parts* Readers can often find small, readable parts in unfamiliar words. Use the following prompts to confirm using word parts to read words.

That word is difficult. Look for a part of the word that you can read. Can you find any other part of the word you can read? Say the parts together.

Page 10 **FOCUS STRATEGY** *Use Context Clues to Confirm Meaning* Readers can use the context of a sentence or passage to identify words. Use the following prompts to confirm using context to identify words.

What word would make sense in this sentence? Think about a word that would make sense and begins and ends as this word does. Now use your word and try the sentence again.

Monitor Comprehension

1. **What did the family do with things they didn't need?** *(They gave some things away, sold some things at a yard sale, and threw some things away.)* **INFERENTIAL: SUMMARIZE**

2. **How did the family celebrate at the end of the day?** *(They had a pizza party.)* **LITERAL: NOTE DETAILS**

3. **How do you think the clean-up day made people happy?** *(Possible responses: People were happy to get the clothes and toys; people were happy with the things they bought at the sale; the family was happy that the house looked great.)* **INFERENTIAL: SPECULATE**

Write in Response to Reading

Explain that people often make posters to advertise a yard sale. Have children write and decorate yard sale posters for this clean-up day.

VOCABULARY LIST

left

scary

share

smiled

something

Henry

by F. R. Robinson

Summary

Henry is a bird that is adopted by a family of lizards. His differences are not always appreciated, but eventually Henry learns he is special.

Introduce the Book

PICTURE WALK Read the title and share the cover. Tell children that Henry is the bird in the picture. Then have them look through the pictures and tell what is happening. Have them read to find out what is special about Henry.
PREDICT/SET PURPOSE

Guided Reading

Page 4   **FOCUS STRATEGY**   *Use Context Clues to Confirm Meaning* Often, the context of a sentence or passage can help readers identify words. Use the following prompts to confirm using context to identify words.

What word do you think would make sense here? Try putting your word in the sentence. Does it make sense now?

Pages 8–9   **FOCUS STRATEGY**   *Look for Word Bits and Parts* Unfamiliar words often contain small parts that children can read. Use the following prompts to help children identify a word by looking at its parts.

That is a tricky word. Look at all the letters. Can you find any part of the word that you can read? Think about the beginning sound. Can you think of a word that begins with this sound and has the part you can read?

Monitor Comprehension

1. **What problems did Henry have because he was different?** *(He had to clean up his feathers; his brothers and sisters thought his wings were scary.)* **INFERENTIAL: SUMMARIZE**

2. **How can you tell that Mother Lizard loves Henry even though he is different?** *(She calls him one of her beautiful babies; she tells him he is special.)* **INFERENTIAL: DETERMINE CHARACTERS' EMOTIONS**

3. **How do you think Henry feels about his lizard family? How can you tell?** *(Possible responses: He loves them. He loves to take them flying.)* **INFERENTIAL: DETERMINE CHARACTERS' EMOTIONS**

Write in Response to Reading

Have children draw a picture of themselves, showing something that makes them special to the people who love and care for them. Encourage them to write a sentence that describes the picture and tells what makes them special.

Silly Aunt Tilly

by Jennifer Jacobson

Summary

Aunt Tilly travels the globe and brings unusual souvenirs to her niece.

Introduce the Book

PICTURE WALK Read the title and share the cover. Have children tell what Aunt Tilly is carrying and why someone would need a suitcase. Have them look through the pictures and tell what Aunt Tilly is doing. Then have them read to find out what Aunt Tilly brings her niece. **PREDICT/SET PURPOSE**

Guided Reading

Page 3 **FOCUS STRATEGY** *Use Picture Clues to Confirm Meaning* Use the following prompts to confirm using pictures to identify words.

Look at the picture. What do you see? What word would help tell about the picture? Say the sentence with your word. Does it make sense?

Page 12 **FOCUS STRATEGY** *Self-Correct* Readers know a word is misread if it does not make sense. They will often correct the word on their own. Use the following prompts to affirm readers who correct their own mistakes.

You first read that as ____ . Then you changed it to ____ . What told you that you should change the word? You did a good job of using clues to figure out what the word should be.

Monitor Comprehension

1. **How did the girl feel about Aunt Tilly's trips?** *(She felt sad because she wanted to go along.)* **INFERENTIAL: DETERMINE CHARACTERS' EMOTIONS**

2. **What do you think the girl might have told her Aunt Tilly?** *(Possible responses: Would you take me with you sometime? I'd like to go with you.)* **CRITICAL: IDENTIFY WITH CHARACTERS**

3. **What do you think the girl and her aunt might do on the moon?** *(Responses will vary.)* **CRITICAL: SPECULATE**

Write in Response to Reading

Have children look through the pictures to notice the stamps or stickers that are added to Aunt Tilly's suitcase each time she takes a trip. Provide them with construction paper to decorate like a suitcase, and have them draw a sticker on the suitcase for a place they might like to go. Then have them write about where they went. They might want to begin with the sentence frame *I went to ____ one day.*

What's New at the Zoo?

by Sharon Fear

Summary

The zookeepers try to figure out why the animals are behaving so strangely. They finally understand when they discover the newest addition to the zoo.

Introduce the Book

PICTURE WALK Read the title and share the cover. Have children guess what might be new at a zoo. Have them look through the pictures, stopping at page 15, and tell what strange things the animals are doing. Then have children read to find out what is new at the zoo. **PREDICT/SET PURPOSE**

Guided Reading

Page 6   **FOCUS STRATEGY**   *Use Context Clues to Confirm Meaning* Readers can often use context to help them identify words. Use the following prompts to confirm using the context to confirm words.

You said ____. Does that make sense? Read the sentence again and think about what word might make sense here. Now try your word.

Page 15   **FOCUS STRATEGY**   *Make Predictions* Use the following prompts to encourage children to make predictions about the story.

What are the animals doing? What could be new and not cause trouble? What do you think the animals and zookeepers are watching?

Monitor Comprehension

1. **How can you tell that Rosa and Al took good care of the animals?** (*Possible responses: They gave them good food and baths. They were worried when the animals acted strangely.*) **METACOGNITIVE: DETERMINE CHARACTERS' TRAITS**

2. **How do you think the animals felt about the new baby?** (*Possible response: They were happy or excited.*) **CRITICAL: IDENTIFY CHARACTERS' EMOTIONS**

3. **What do you think the animals were saying to each other?** (*Responses will vary.*) **CRITICAL: SPECULATE**

Write in Response to Reading

Tell children that zoos are very proud of new baby animals. Have them think of a name for this baby, and then ask children to make a poster inviting people to come see the new baby at the zoo.

The Strongest One of All

retold by Y. Kim Choi

Summary

In this retelling of a Korean folktale, two parents learn that there are many different kinds of strength.

Introduce the Book

PICTURE WALK Read the title and share the cover. Explain that this is a story from a faraway country called Korea. Have children look through the pages and tell who they see the mice talking to in each picture. Then have them read to find out how the mice find the strongest one of all. **PREDICT/SET PURPOSE**

Guided Reading

Page 4 **FOCUS STRATEGY** *Use Context Clues to Confirm Meaning* When an unfamiliar word is encountered, readers can determine the word from its meaning in context. Use the following prompts to encourage using context to confirm words.

You hesitated, and then you said ____. Does that make sense? What clues helped you figure out the word?

Page 10 **FOCUS STRATEGY** *Self-Correct* When a misread word interrupts the meaning of the text, readers will make the needed correction on their own. The following prompts will help affirm children correcting themselves.

After you said ____, you changed the word to ____. How did you know that the first word was wrong? How did you know what word was right?

Monitor Comprehension

1. **What did the sun, the cloud, and the wind tell the mice?** *(Each one told the mice that someone else was stronger than they were.)* **INFERENTIAL: SUMMARIZE**

2. **Why did the mice ask a mouse to marry their daughter?** *(The statue told them that a mouse could dig a hole and make it fall over.)* **INFERENTIAL: SUMMARIZE**

3. **Why do you think the daughter was so happy?** *(Possible response: She wanted to marry a mouse all along.)* **CRITICAL: DETERMINE CHARACTERS' EMOTIONS**

Write in Response to Reading

Work with children to brainstorm a list of strong things, such as a rock or a wave. Then, as you name each thing on the list, have them tell what might be stronger. Have children choose something from the list and write and illustrate one or more sentences telling what is stronger and why.

Individual Reading Inventory Summary Form

Student: _____ Grade: _____ Date: _____

Passage: _____ Word Count: _____

1. Miscues

Total number of miscues _____

    Meaning-based miscues _____

    Graphic/sound-based miscues _____

Comments and patterns observed: _____

_____

Total number of self-corrections _____

Comments and patterns observed: _____

_____

Error Rate

- Subtract the number of self-corrections from the total number of miscues for a subtotal.
- Divide the subtotal by the word count of the passage.

_____ ÷ _____ = _____

(SUBTOTAL)   **(WORD COUNT)**   **ERROR RATE**

2. Fluency

Number of words read per minute _____

_____ ÷ _____ = _____

(NUMBER OF CORRECT   **(WORD COUNT)**   **FLUENCY RATE**
WORDS READ PER MINUTE)

Comments and patterns observed: _____

_____

3. Comprehension

_____ ÷ **4 X 100** = _____%

(TOTAL CORRECT ANSWERS)   **COMPREHENSION SCORE**

Comments and patterns observed: _____

_____

Summary Comments

Individual Reading
Inventory Form

Student: _____   Date: _____

Selection Title: *My book*   Word Count: 17

My gate

My door

My bathroom

My bedroom

My cupboard

My bed

My book

My light

Goodnight

Comments: _____

_____

_____

Indicate correct (+) or incorrect (-) response for each question:

1. Where is the first place we see the cat? (at the gate)

2. Where does he go next? (the door)

3. What do you think he will find in the house? (Possible response: people)

4. Who is in the bedroom? (the child telling the story)

Individual Reading Inventory Form

Student: _____   Date: _____

Selection Title: *Five Little Ducks*, pages 1–17   Word Count: 108

Five little ducks went out one day,
Over the hills and far away.

Mother Duck said,
"Quack, quack, quack, quack."

But only four little ducks came back.

Four little ducks went out one day,
Over the hills and far away.

Mother Duck said,
"Quack, quack, quack, quack."

But only three little ducks came back.

Three little ducks went out one day,
Over the hills and far away.

Mother Duck said,
"Quack, quack, quack, quack."

But only two little ducks came back.

Two little ducks went out one day,
Over the hills and far away.

Mother Duck said,
"Quack, quack, quack, quack."

But only one little duck came back.

Comments: _____

_____

Indicate correct (+) or incorrect (-) response for each question:

1. **Where did the ducks go?** (over the hills and far away)

2. **How many ducks stayed over the hills and far away each time?** (one duck)

3. **Why do you think Mother Duck said, "Quack, quack, quack, quack"?** (to tell her ducklings to follow her)

4. **How many ducks do you think will come back the next time?** (none)

Individual Reading
Inventory Form

Student: _____ Date: _____

Selection Title: *"Pardon?" Said the Giraffe*, pages 1–11   Word Count: 106

"What's it like up there?"
asked the frog as he hopped on the ground.

"Pardon?" said the giraffe.

"What's it like up there?"
asked the frog as he hopped on the lion.

"Pardon?" said the giraffe.

"What's it like up there?"
asked the frog as he hopped on the hippo.

"Pardon?" said the giraffe.

"What's it like up there?"
asked the frog as he hopped on the elephant.

"Pardon?" said the giraffe.

"What's it like up there?"
asked the frog as he hopped on the giraffe.

"It's nice up here, thank you," said the giraffe,
"but you're tickling my nose and I think I'm going to . . ."

Comments: _____

_____

_____

Indicate correct (+) or incorrect (-) response for each question:

1. **What question does the frog keep asking?** ("What's it like up there?")

2. **Who is he speaking to?** (the giraffe)

3. **Who is the last animal the frog hops onto?** (the giraffe)

4. **What might happen since the frog is tickling the giraffe's nose?** (The giraffe might sneeze.)

Individual Reading Inventory Form

Student: _____   Date: _____

Selection Title: *Two Bear Cubs*   Word Count: 103

Six bright eyes look out of a dark cave.

A bear and her cubs begin their day.

The mother watches while her cubs play.

Something walks by.
It doesn't smell like a bear.

The cubs follow it.

It follows them!

At last they outrun it.
But where are they?

And where is their mother?

They look around.
They sniff the ground.

No mother.

They find a honey tree all by themselves—

and a lot of angry bees!
Where is their mother?

They can't even catch a fish.
Where can their mother be?

There she is!

And they aren't even very far from home.

Comments: _____

_____

_____

Indicate correct (+) or incorrect (-) response for each question:

1. **How many bears are in the story?** (three—a mother bear and her two cubs)

2. **What is the first thing that the cubs see?** (a skunk)

3. **What happens when the bears find the honey tree?** (They find honey, but they also get chased by the bees.)

4. **Does the mother bear really leave her cubs all alone?** (No, she is watching them from a distance.)

Individual Reading
Inventory Form

Student: _____   Date: _____

Selection Title: *Leo the Late Bloomer*, pages 1–16   Word Count: 109

Leo couldn't do anything right.

He couldn't read.

He couldn't write.

He couldn't draw.

He was a sloppy eater.

And, he never said a word.

"What's the matter with Leo?"
asked Leo's father.
"Nothing," said Leo's mother.
"Leo is just a late bloomer."
"Better late than never," thought Leo's father.

Every day Leo's father watched him
for signs of blooming.

And every night Leo's father watched him
for signs of blooming.

"Are you sure Leo's a bloomer?" asked Leo's father.
"Patience," said Leo's mother.
"A watched bloomer doesn't bloom."

So Leo's father watched television instead of Leo.

The snows came.
Leo's father wasn't watching.
But Leo still wasn't blooming.

Comments: _____

_____

Indicate correct (+) or incorrect (–) response for each question:

1. What is Leo's problem? (He is a late bloomer.)

2. Who is more worried about Leo, his mother or his father? (his father)

3. How do you know this? (His father keeps watching for signs of blooming.)

4. What does Leo's mother tell his father to do? (Have patience.)

Individual Reading Inventory Form

Student: _____   Date: _____

Selection Title: *The Art Lesson*, pages 1–5   Word Count: 110

Tommy knew he wanted to be an artist when he grew up.

He drew pictures everywhere he went. It was his favorite thing to do.

His friends had favorite things to do, too.

Jack collected all kinds of turtles.

Herbie made huge cities in his sandbox.

Jeannie, Tommy's best friend, could do cartwheels and stand on her head.

But Tommy drew and drew and drew.

His twin cousins, who were already grown up, were in art school learning to be real artists.

They told him not to copy and to practice, practice, practice. So, he did.

Tommy put his pictures up on the walls of his half of the bedroom.

Comments: _____

_____

_____

Indicate correct (+) or incorrect (-) response for each question:

1. **What does Tommy want to be when he grows up?** (an artist)

2. **Do Tommy's friends like to draw as much as he does?** (No, they like to collect things, play in the sandbox, and do cartwheels.)

3. **What does Tommy think is special about his cousins?** (They are in art school.)

4. **What advice do they give Tommy?** (not to copy and to practice, practice, practice)

Reading Log

Student's Name

Emergent

The Three Bears										
A Day at School										
At Home										
My book*										
The Pet Store										
All Fall Down										
Butterflies										
Garden Birthday										
My Dog										
Old MacDonald's Fun Time Farm										
The Baby										
What a Shower!										
Have You Seen My Cat?										
Good-bye, Fox										
I Like Food										
Just Like You!										
My Sister Is My Friend										
Spring Pops Up										
The Perfect Pet										
We Are Friends										
What Could It Be?										
Where Babies Play										
Bird's Bad Day										
"Help!" Said Jed										
Friendship Salad										
My Family Band										
One More Time										
Play Ball!										
What Time Is It?										
Five Little Ducks*										
After Goldilocks										
Know Your Birthday Manners										

*Benchmark Book

Reading Log

Early

Happy Birthday											
One Little Slip											
Today Is Monday											
What Is in the Box?											
Famous Feet											
Five Little Monkeys Jumping on the Bed											
"Pardon?" Said the Giraffe*											
All I Did											
Pet Day											
Four Very Big Beans											
Look What I Can Read!											
Every Cat											
A Place for Nicholas											
Frog's Day											
Biscuit											
Lost and Found											
My Wild Woolly											
The King Who Loved to Dance											
The Little Chicks Sing											
The Night Walk											
What's Up?											
Sid and Sam											
Let's Visit the Moon											
I Was Just About to Go to Bed											
The Green Grass Grows All Around											
Red											
Big Brown Bear											
Alien Vacation											
Dancing											
Green Green Green											
Two Bear Cubs*											
Slowpoke Snail											
Lunch in Space											
Pet Riddles and Jokes with Franny and Frank											
Davy Crockett and the Wild Cat											
If You Were a Bat											
Plenty of Pets											
Dream Around the World											
Henry											
How 100 Dandelions Grew											

*Benchmark Book

Reading Log

Fluent	Student's Name											
Silly Aunt Tilly												
How to Make a Lion Mask												
Shoe Town												
Skimper-Scamper												
Leo the Late Bloomer*												
Clean-Up Day												
Fire Fighters												
How the Sky Got Its Stars												
What's New at the Zoo?												
Ask Mr. Bear												
Hare's Big Tug-of-War												
The Big Dipper												
The Strongest One of All												
Peeping and Sleeping												
Little Fox Goes to the End of the World												
Leon and Bob												
The Art Lesson*												
Four Fur Feet												
Henry and Mudge and the Happy Cat												
How a Seed Grows												
Listen Buddy												
Man on the Moon												

*Benchmark Book